First Published in the United States of America

Copyright © 2020 King Ari Dane
All Rights Reserved.

ISBN: 979-8646913099

DISCLAIMER

Table of Contents

Introduction

When it comes to money, there are two rules. Rule number one: never lose money. Rule number two: Never forget the first rule.

Each one of us has different amounts of money, and I'm not just talking about our bank account balance but all liquid or near-liquid assets we have. All of these assets qualify to be called the money that we have. By the time you are finished with this book, the rules discussed above will be ingrained in your mind and the way you deal with finances. As you read, you will learn the various aspects of personal finance and practical tips to improve your financial condition. But before you start off, you need to know the "why" of personal finance.

When we talk about money management, the term is typically used to point out the financial management of resources that belong to an individual or a family. It comprises various aspects, ranging from how you manage your expenditure, savings, and investments, while simultaneously taking into account the possibility of different life events and risks. Other facets of personal finance are banking, budgeting, insurance, retirement planning, and more. The term, money management, can also refer to the involvement of the financial industry in your life; all institutions offering financial services are part of the financial sector.

The focus of managing your money is primarily on you and what caters to your financial goals, both in the long and short-term. As the famous quote goes, "A wise man has money in his head, not his heart." Financial literacy is a critical trait of a wise person; it helps him or her to distinguish between the financial decisions that will be detrimental or beneficial for their monetary future. Planning your finances will enable you to achieve your short and long-term goals, all without exceeding your income limits.

The sooner you start to manage your money, the better.

How To Manage Your Money That You Already Have

Chapter 1 – Knowing Where You Stand

When you are trying to find your way, it is often better to get to higher ground. The elevated ground will offer you a good vantage point to figure your way to where you want to go. This analogy helps us understand that we need to know where we currently are; so that we know the direction we need to head in to reach our destination.

For some of us, facing our financial situation can be a little unnerving and even frightening; this might also be true for you, given that you have come around to read this book. When you bring your financial state to your awareness, your train of thought automatically takes you to think of ways you can improve your situation. When you start thinking of money, it is a tough task to stop thinking that lifestyle changes and significant sacrifices are your only way out. However, it does not matter how scary your financial position is because the only way you can improve your circumstances is by confronting and thoroughly assessing them. The good news is that this chapter is all about teaching you how.

Evaluating your financial position is a step-wise procedure. Before you face the calculated facts about the money you have, it's a herculean task to develop the self-discipline and resolve that you require to implement your plan. We begin with a fact-finding exercise; you ask yourself some specific questions to write down a summary of your circumstances. The more the bad news you get as you move through this evaluation procedure, the more it alerts you to get committed to managing your money. In this way, the financial position evaluation process can serve as a measure of the time and effort you need to invest in managing your money. As soon as you are done with the evaluation, the faster and more straightforward it'll be to better your finances.

Let's start!

Questions You Need to Ask Yourself

When you need to find out your personal financial situation, who knows it better than you? But even though you are the only person with the most considerable amount of information about your finances, you might not have the skills to gauge them accurately. This is why many people hire personal accountants, book-keeping services, and whatnot just to manage their money. You can perfectly manage your money by yourself, you just need a little guidance, so you know the steps you need to take.

Managing the money, you already have has one central aspect: self-evaluation. The better you are at self-evaluation, the better your understanding of your money.

Not taking much of your time to discuss theories or ideas, we'll move to the action part straightaway. When you are answering the questions, some questions will be based on your opinion rather than facts and numbers. So, to answer these questions, you are advised to stay true to yourself and be optimistic!

To answer these questions, you are required to research. Also, it needs introspection about your goals and what you value in life; this is why you need to be true to yourself. The process of answering these questions is going to be a blessing in disguise. By the time you will be able to respond to a question logically, you will have fresh insight into the situation and a new perspective.

What are my sources of income?

You probably know the total amount of money that you make in a year or the amount of annual taxable income. You would even know how much you earn per hour from your day job, but are you aware of your monthly net income? You also need to identify the different sources of income for you.

For example, your sources of income may be your primary job, a side hustle that you keep, or the rent from the house that you have leased.

Search up your latest salary bill and check what your total salary was. Check both the original amount of income before any tax deductions, healthcare insurance, retirement savings, and the net take-home income after all deductions. Do the same for all of your identified sources of income, so you get a concise summary of your monthly income.

Furthermore, if you live with your spouse and combine your finances, consider the sum of income for both of you.

How much do I save?

Savings is the part of your income that is not used for current expenses. Savings are important because you do not know what is going to happen in the future. Hence, you should save money to pay for unexpected occasions or emergencies. Your car may breakdown, your dishwasher may start leaking, or a medical emergency emerges. Without enough savings, these emergency situations become enormous financial burdens. You need to see the amount you have left after fulfilling all the expenses for a month this then could be your savings.

Use a savings calculator to figure out the amount of money that you should save each month and compare it with the average amount of money that you do save. There will be some of us that fail entirely to make any savings, but that is not a thing to worry about. This book will help you to go from no savings at all, to more savings than you need.

Am I on the right savings pace so I can do well after retirement?

Answering this question is not as easy as it seems, because retirement has different meanings for different people. This question needs both: genuine introspection and research. An online savings calculator is a great way to determine the amount of money you need to put away. Hence, you have enough resources to do what you want by the time you retire.

Most importantly you need to know to answer these questions:

What is your current income?

Who are the people who you are saving for? Is it only you or your family too?

What is your desired retirement age?

What do you want to accomplish with the retirement savings, how long do you expect them to last after you retire?

Once you are sure of these things, you'll have the primary inputs to help you to decide a realistic figure that you should save to get the exact type of retirement you want. You might not be motivated enough to save for your old age now. Still, a word of advice from experts: You certainly don't want to have your financial goals unattained in your retirement, to play catch up your entire life.

When was the last time I lost money, and why?

Money mistakes are most commonly spending mistakes: when you spend your money somewhere, and it ends up getting wasted. In other words, any action that leads you to lose money that you would've had otherwise qualifies for a money mistake. When you identify the last time, you lost money what happens is, your train of thought enables you to identify other instances where you had lost money. You then figure out the most common way that you lose money.

The second part of answering this question, is figuring out why you made this mistake. What landed you in the situation that caused you to spend your money in nonsensically – or sometimes you can also lose money without making a mistake. So, what you should think about is: Did you lose money because of the emotional state you were in? Was it the people around you? Was it the place you were at? Figuring out these things will help you stop this from happening again.

Do I have a plan if I am suddenly unemployed?

When you are let go from your job, some of the issues that come to your mind right away are: How am I going to get re-employed? And how can I replace my previous source of income? But all these things come after figuring out how you are going to sustain yourself and sustain the means of support for you family before you get back to work. The emergency fund makes an entry over here. You should prioritize saving a sum of money exclusively for emergency purposes.

Do I have enough in my emergency fund?

Experts argue that you should have at least $1000 in your emergency fund. Others say that the amount should be no more or less than three months' worth of your fixed expenses. You may be confusing your emergency fund with your savings; although your savings can act as your emergency fund, a more financially accomplished person always keeps their emergency fund separate from their savings.

When you have a separate emergency fund and a separate savings fund, you are less likely to use the savings fund bit by bit. What usually happens is that when you have no other option but to take from your savings in times of emergency, it eventually becomes a casual thing to take from your savings every now and then.

How much do I have in debt?

Debt is not something that we can be proud of or even face without worrying. There are different types of debts, like student loans, credit card debt, or simple bank loans. Hiding or running away from what you owe does not make things any better; you can escape the stress for a while, but it eventually is going to hit you harder the next time around. Thus, it is better to face the music and handle things while you still have time. Facing your debt feels like an emotional challenge, but by doing so, and then taking practical steps towards paying them off, your world will be a whole lot better.

Reflect on any debt that you have acquired in the past, no matter how small or big. Include the money you have borrowed from family or friends, make a list, and ascertain the amount of debt you still have and how much you are paying towards debt every month.

Do I have a plan to pay off debt?

Paying off debt with the money you have will be discussed later in the book. However, you still need to ask yourself this question now. Do you have a plan or not? And if not, it only adds to the urgency of devoting more time and effort to improve your finances. If you do have a plan, well and good! You will only benefit more as you read the upcoming chapters.

What large expenses am I expecting in the future?

When managing money, it is essential to anticipate the large payments that are coming in the next few years. Rather than stressing and panicking when those enormous bills knock on your door, a much better and stress-free approach is to save, starting now.

For instance, you have a $5,000 property tax coming in ten months. By answering this question, you will have anticipated the upcoming payment, and you can start putting aside $500 each month to have the payment ready on time. This not only leads you to be mentally prepared but also makes the payment process seamless.

Am I losing sleep over money?

A "yes" to this question means that you need to start taking steps now, practical measures. If this is the case, you need to change your mindset. You need to understand that money is a tool, not a consequence; you will learn more about this later. What you need to know now is that taking the right steps towards a better financial position is an excellent stress-reliever in itself.

Evaluating Your Relationship with Money

Before we go into greater depth, why not understand what we mean by your relationship with money. How you relate to, or how you emotionally feel about money makes up the most part of your relationship with money. Your mindset about money and how it affects your life is the other part. Simply put, your relationship with money is how money makes you feel, or how you perceive money can change you.

Your relationship with money mainly impacts how well you are going to be at managing your money. Here are some examples of an unhealthy relationship with money:

Having the misconception that money determines how happy you are, or you are what you buy. You might believe this to some extent that the greater the amount of money you spend, the more successful or influential you are in the eyes of others. Acquiring this mindset is too easy in the modern world with widespread social media and advertising campaigns that equate money with success or happiness in life.

There are some psychological and philosophical issues about money and its value in life. There are people who don't save at all, and there are people who spend their whole lives in the pursuit of saving more money and increasing their net worth; either of these extremes is no good. Many people attribute way too much significance to accumulating personal wealth while neglecting the things in life for which money is saved in the first place. Retirees get addicted to saving, and spending money in large amounts after retirement seems like an impossible task for them. They hinder themselves from actually spending the money they worked hard to save for spending when the time comes.

There are four types of people when it comes to money, and your type is also the relationship you have with money.

Spenders: Spenders like money. Spenders like to spend money. And spenders spend money, expecting that their money is going to bring them happiness. They will often make purchases that are more than what they can afford and will accumulate credit card debts.

Misers: Misers like money. Misers like to save money. Surprisingly, spenders and misers are like the two opposite extremes, and yet they have one thing in common: the desire for wealth. Maybe the problem is with this desire for wealth.

Haters: Haters hate money. They like to stay away from money. Such people argue that money brings unhappiness and dissatisfaction to people and corrupts society.

Seekers: Seekers are people who primarily emphasize on becoming rich. They don't have a saving or spending tendency; instead, they have the mindset that their resources are their source of happiness. In most cases, such people are trying to make up for other shortcomings in life with their riches.

Frankly speaking, none of these four types is perfect, and neither are you. So, let's accept the type we fall into, and let's see beyond money. Let's work towards suppressing our imperfections to attain a balance.

How to use your Credit Score?

The credit score is one indicator of where you stand financially. Also known as the FICO score, the score enumerates how responsible you are when it comes to finances.

The credit score determines if you can acquire loans, and other businesses judge your candidacy for various purposes based on credit score too. Ranging from landing a job to renting a new place to live, your credit score directly impacts all. Here are some of the terms you need to be familiar with to understand the concept of credit fully:

Credit History: This is the record of your past payments of bills and other liabilities. It records all the clearances that you have made. It records whether you made those payments on time or not. It records all the deposits you haven't made and the amount of debt you have on you at present.

Credit Report: This is a summary of your credit history collected from different sources, like your insurance company, your bank, and other financial institutions. It helps give a more vivid perspective on your credit situation and whether you make your payments responsibly or not.

Credit score: The information in your credit report and other data about you, such as the property you own, your bank statements, and your family data, are then summed up in a special mathematical algorithm to determine your credit score. 35% of the credit score is made up of payment history, 30% is derived from the total amount you owe presently, 15% depends on how your credit history is, the longer it is, the better. The remaining 20% is based on the combination of the credit types and new credit; this represents the recent loan applications you have made. The range of credit scores is 300 to 850; while scores above 700 are good and 800 are excellent, any score lower than 580 represents bad credit.

Three national credit companies are operating in the United States: Experion, Equifax, and TransUnion. You can get your credit report from all three of them and get valuable information about your financial position instantly.

It is your right to obtain one copy of your credit report free every year. For a thorough and comprehensive evaluation, order one copy from each of the three national credit agencies, and not just from one. Each of the reports might contain slightly varying information, because all creditors do not report all of the consumer account payment data to all three companies.

Frequent checks on your credit reports ensure that you are aware of your finances. Checking them is crucial because the credit score or report is going to be what future creditors, employers, or landlords are going to use to assess your candidacy. When you are already aware of your credit, you can take steps to improve it, so you do not face any inconvenience in the future.

Your credit score is one figure that can either cost or save you a great deal of money. An excellent score of 800+ can land you lower interest rates on your debt; this means any line of credit you take out will cost you less. On the other hand, a lower credit means the interest would be high, and loans will be expensive. However, it is entirely up to you to ensure your credit remains excellent, so you have a variety of options when you need to borrow money. If you stand anywhere below 650 on the credit score index, you should be alarmed.

Comparing What You Own VS. What You Owe

One route that you can take to determine where you stand is to weigh what you own and what you owe. Sometimes the line of division between the two can get a little hazy, and it gets tough to assess your circumstances. By practicing the following fact-check exercise, you will have a more unobstructed view of your financial status.

The assets that you own can be but are not limited to, the following:
Real estate
Bank accounts
Stocks and Bonds (brokerage accounts)
Pensions
Retirement accounts
Cars, boats, and other vehicles
Jewelry
Household items
Furniture, computers, and phones
Debts include:
Mortgages

Credit card accounts
Student loans
Vehicle loans
Unsecured loans
Loans from your 401K, IRA, or other retirement accounts

Most people can figure out or agree on fair ways to divide their debts and assets. If you have a complicated asset, you might want to talk with an expert. Similarly, you may need to seek legal advice if you have a marital property that you are having trouble dividing.

Once you have cleared all doubts and uncertainties, now it is time to assign the monetary values to each part of the lists mentioned above. Assigning monetary values to non-liquid items such as household items can be a tough job. It may consume a lot of time, but the benefits that will accrue to you from this comparison are worth the effort. Also, you will have to consider the total cost of a debt, which includes the interest till the time you expect to pay off the loan. It is better to consider the uncertainty in the value of your debts and assets. For instance, if you are unsure of what the cost of a long-term loan might be in the future, you should assign it a value range.

The sum of the monetary value of your assets and the sum of the monetary value for your debts will then paint a picture that is easy for you to interpret. If the value of your debt is more than the value of your assets, you have a negative net worth. Your net worth will provide you with a snapshot of your current financial situation. When you calculate your net worth, you will be able to see the final result of all your financial actions, all that you've earned, and all that you've spent to date. Furthermore, by calculating your net worth frequently, you can use the change in your net worth as a report that can help you evaluate the results of different financial practices. Not only will you figure out your financial health, but it will also help you figure out what steps you need to take to achieve your financial goals. Negative net worth does not always refer to bankruptcy. The value of assets can quickly plunge, but they can also rise at the same pace. For example, when the 2008 financial crisis began to recede, the prices of residential property rose, and people who owned homes quickly saw their net worth go from negative figures to positive.

How To Manage Your Money That You Already Have

Chapter 2 – Change the Way you Look at Money

What do we mean when we talk about changing the way we look at or think about money? People are sinking in debt and poor financial conditions now more than ever, and there are only a handful of people that are genuinely successful in managing their money. So, what does this imply? It's clear that most of the people that find themselves in financial conditions do not think about money in the right way, or they don't have the right mindset.

Building wealth and managing money have more to do with your mindset than you might think. Just as we have relationships with the people in our life, money is a part of our life, and we have a relationship with money too. The way you earn your money, the way you spend it, waste it, lose it, or save it; all of these constitute your relationship with money. It is essential to take a good look at the way you use and misuse your money. If you do not, you will never really be able to get a good grip on what happens to your money, and more often than not, you'll be left confused, contemplating what happened to your money.

In this chapter, you will learn about the mindset you should have to manage your money well, not only this but also what you can do to improve your mindset. Finding common ground on your finances can also be difficult when one partner is shopaholic, and the other one's a miser; most of you are not in this boat alone. Along with yourself, educating your spouse is essential because living a financially smart life is a choice lived simpler when both partners are on the same page about their general financial goals. If both of you want to save your money, pay off your debts, and live a financially stress-free life, you need to discuss the way you think about money management and find common ground. Any efforts that you make can be rendered useless if your partner or family members stay on the same spending habits as they had before.

Money is a Tool, Not a Consequence

Whether you acknowledge it or not, a large proportion of your time is spent thinking of money and how we can have more of it. You might wish you had more money, you may think of how much you spend on different things, hear about the financial market in the news; our mind is bombarded with the same money-related information when we blame our family wasting money, when we request for a better paycheck, and so on. How we live our lives and the way we stress about money every day has led us to think that money is a result, something that we want to achieve.

Because we spend so much of our time thinking about money, we rubbish the fact that money is only a tool, it is only an aid to help us achieve the real things in life. There is a reason you hear some people saying that money cannot buy happiness, they say this because their goal was to get more and more money, and they were eventually disappointed. Money is not something that will satisfy you.

On the other hand, if you realize that money is what aids you to satisfy your needs and achieve your goals, then you will see that money does contribute to happiness. This is because money is not the final goal; it is merely an instrument that aids us in achieving what we deem to be a better future. Money is a tool, not a result.

Thinking this way is going to help you regardless of what money category you belong to or the type of relationship you have with money. If you are a miser, then it may help you realize the fact that saving money forever is not going to help you at all, unless you spend it for utility. If you are a money seeker, it may help you to realize that you should seek what intrinsically makes you happy rather than money. Money indeed is what enables us to get what we want; however, our mindset should not be to achieve money; rather, it should be how to achieve our goal? Money comes in the path to our destination but should never be the destination.

Having a Vision

Your vision is a goal that you imagine; it is a mission for you underpinned by moral inspiration. On the other hand, an ideal is only something that you want to be or have; it does not have a why. Here are some examples that will help you differentiate between the two:

Ideal. I want to be a millionaire. Vision: I want to be rich so that I can help the homeless.

The difference between the two is that the vision is meaningful; it has a 'why' that tells you the logic behind it. When you do not have logic behind an ideal and when you do not have a 'why,' you would get bored of working for it sooner than you think. A vision, on the contrary, can boost you for years. With a sound and logical 'why,' you will easily figure out the 'how.'

For example, when you have a monthly budget, it can assist you in consolidating your vision as you will clearly see where your money is going and where you would like it to go. So rather than saying, "I need to save," you should say, "I need to save so I can take my spouse on a vacation." By simply changing the way you talk about money, you can gradually change the way you think about it. Always keep yourself aware of the fact that money is the route, not the target.

Concentrate on the Good Things

This one practical tip to change the way you think of money comes from the extremely basic personal development rule: concentrate on the solution, not the problem.

The problem with most people is that they tend to focus all their efforts on the negative things. They get fixated to paying off their debt or paying their long-due rent, and it becomes just like a central theme of their life. Because they think so much about debt and bills, most of their attention or efforts, regarding finance, is aimed only to achieve the lowest target – just managing to reduce debt or bills.

Yes, of course, reducing debt and paying bills is nothing terrible, and you should do it responsibly. We are only asking you to not let these things bog you down or allow them to distract you from being wealthier. This is the primary reason why you may hear financial experts advising their clients to get an automatic debt payment service, so you can focus on achieving your other life goals.

The principle behind this phenomenon is the law of attraction. It states that the more you think of something, the more you attract it. Similarly, the more you think about debt and paying it off, the more you attract debt and vice versa.

Like will always attracts like. You cannot attract money in your life unless you think, act, and talk like wealthy people. Acting wealthy does not mean that you go on a spending spree and spend a lot of money that you may not even have at the moment. Acting wealthy means to allow yourself to window shop and plan for expensive things, plan long holidays, treat yourself to little luxuries from time to time. The more you feel like you have already manifested your desires, the faster they will actually manifest in your life. So, find little ways by which you can begin living your dreams right now. If you hope to find your soulmate, you should feel like you are loved, admire yourself, and compliment yourself. If you dream of having a lot of money, wear your best clothes and have a productive attitude. When you are encountered by a situation where you have to spend a lot of cash, do not think that you can't afford it, think about how you can afford it. This is an example of having a problem-solving attitude. If you dream of traveling, explore the places that are near you, your own city, and experience new things.

21

These little actions will make a massive impact on the way the Law of Attraction affects you. Begin to inculcate a new feeling and vibration inside yourself, which will consequently manifest your desires.

Not Letting Emotions Take Over You

If you have lived a financially tight early life or have grown up not with a lot of resources, you might have developed a firm negative emotional perception regarding money.

By most of the world's population, money has always been viewed as a source of anxiety and stress. People's everyday experiences regarding money directly indicates whether they are going to have a good day or not. These kinds of people strongly feel that their self-worth or self-esteem is directly impacted by what kind of clothes they wear, how beautiful their house is, or what type of vehicle they own. All of these things point back to one common thing, the money they have in their banks. Money should not be allowed to have such significance in our life that it can directly impact how we feel emotionally or decide our self-worth.

As we have discussed before, if we can view our money as just a tool for us to use and nothing more, we take charge of our lives and not the money.

We certainly let money take over our emotions, and if we allow money to control us and our actions, how can we use it as a tool? If you still are not convinced that money is just a tool, just like a hammer, or a vacuum cleaner or a keyboard, you should be. None of us get emotional over a device like a drill machine, do we? The same goes for money because it is nothing more than a tool. Emotions will only cloud your judgment and lead you to make poor choices with money.

If you still think that wealth is success, so hear it from the wealthiest people in the world; they say, "Don't get emotional about money." Following this advice is tough for most of us, and it can be said easily, but the words are right, and the advice is reliable. You should learn to bring money down from the emotional pedestal and place it in your hands, which is an ideal place for a tool. It is essential for you to get into the driver's seat and take yourself towards wealth creation.

Chapter 3 – Some More Advice

If you're getting bored with all these life lessons and theories, and you're waiting to read about some practical stuff, then please be just a little more patient. We have time for all that budgeting and saving tips, but more importantly, having the right mindset and knowing how to deal with problems is a must for you if you want to make your efforts successful. Here are four life-saving advice, read, internalize, and remember. Remember them, so you know what you need to do when such times come.

Believing in Yourself

It is a famous statement; your net worth shows your self-worth. The way you perceive yourself can immensely impact the amount of money you have in your pockets. Someone who believes in himself or herself and realizes how much they can achieve, they begin to act in a way that they can pursue what they want and increase their financial success; this is all because they are more confident in taking the steps that move them closer to their goals. The purpose of emphasizing so much on how you think about money is because all of it starts with having the right mindset and believing in yourself.

Studies have shown that people who are high earners or are living successful lives all have a high level of self-worth. All these people are confident about themselves and advise all people to do the same. Surprisingly, most of these rich people previously thought that they were not able or worthy enough to achieve so much and be so wealthy. Still, they had to conquer this aspect before they could move on to lead successful lives.

If you are reading this and you still doubt in your mind whether you would be able to accomplish your financial goals or not, you should stop right here and make a firm decision. Decide to do all that is in your power to get what you want, and that you would do it by any means.

Let us suppose, for a moment, that you don't believe in yourself that you can be successful. That being the case, you probably don't think you can ever be successful in your financial life. When you believe this, you will not take the steps towards being financially successful like saving, investing, or seeking the advice of financial advisors or even reading this book. So, we know that you have that spark in you, you do have the self-belief that with a little guidance, you will accomplish your goals. Furthermore, you need to change the negative beliefs you have about yourself if you have any; identifying them is the trickier part. If you don't change these negative beliefs, you might behave in ways that aren't beneficial for you and may lead you to think more negatively about yourself!

Working With your Family
You might want to skip this chapter if you live alone. Still, like most people who live with their husbands or wives and their family, you must read this piece if you want to benefit from this book to the full extent.

Four wheels drive a car. Imagine one wheel trying to push the car forward while the other three are jammed in place, or even pushing the car in the opposite direction; what is going to happen? Not only will the vehicle not progress an inch, the one wheel will damage itself and the rest of the car in the process of trying. This analogy perfectly describes the situation where one member of the family is trying to smartly manage their money to drive towards a better future financial situation, but the rest of the family is not helping. When your partner, children, or any family member is not making an effort in the same direction as you, or actually doing the opposite by taking undesirable financial steps, they are, in fact, nullifying all your efforts. Without having your family on board, you are better off not even trying. Just like the one odd wheel will damage itself while it tries to move the wheel forward, you will lead yourself to nothing but extra stress and a waste of time. So, what is the solution?

While you are attaining the financial education, you need as you read this book, make certain that the rest of your family is at the same level of financial literacy. You might want to recommend your partner to read this book along with you, or you can gather your family and have a meeting. You can tell your family the vital information they need to have, such as wise spending, budgeting, and saving. The goal is to deliver the following message effectively: "I need my family to support me in securing a better future for themselves by taking wise and educated steps in managing the money we already have."

There are a variety of steps you can take to educate your family about their finances. Family meetings, appointments with financial advisors, life lessons, and the list goes on. However, if you have this book, you only need the knowledge in this book and a bit of talking to get yourself and your family ready to travel on the road to success. One choice is to recommend your partner to read this book, if they are reluctant, you can suggest to them the specific chapters you think they need to and know the most about. If you still can't get them to read, just talk to them about what you've learned, and you'll surely succeed.

If you have children, you can ask them to read about finances if they are old enough. Although all chapters in this book won't be as entertaining or useful for the kids, you can tell them which parts they need to read as a must. If your children are too young to understand this book, the job is even easier for you. Engage your kids in educative games and lessons, and you are good to go.

How to Deal with Setbacks

Even the best financial experts and advisors out there make financial mistakes and are afflicted with major setbacks, so thinking that once you are financially educated, and you won't suffer a loss again in your life would be wrong. Yes, you will lower the chances of experiencing future losses, but preparedness and knowledge will only take you so far. You are a human, and as a human, you are still going to fault at some point. So, ready yourself to clean the mess up if something of the sort ever happens. You won't be able to reverse time, but there are some things you can do to minimize the damages.

Don't Panic: If you are likely to overspend when you are stressed or take financially risky steps hoping to recover faster from a setback, you could potentially be clearing the path for even more financial problems into your life. You should try to take emotion out of the frame when you are faced with such a situation and seek a solution. Never try to make yourself feel good better about the damages by neglecting or ignoring the mistake you made if any. Instead, you should accept it comfortably and recognize it, so you don't repeat. Focus on practical solutions such as working to earn some extra income or cutting back your expenses.

Seek Help: If you are stressed or having a tough time focusing on what should be done to deal with a setback, you should immediately reach out for support from trusted friends, family, or an advisor. Don't be afraid of asking for assistance. Pick up the phone, call up a financial expert or advisor, and talk to them about your problem. Remember keeping it all in your mind and not talking to anyone about the issue and the solution to it, only make you more emotionally stressed.

Identify your losses: A financial setback often brings plenty of damages or losses with itself. More often than not, setbacks like these comprise of several smaller problems. So, taking the bull by its horns is not a very good option here. You need to thoroughly assess the situation; try to have a good idea of the total losses you have incurred. Only when you enlist the damages, you can start figuring out a plan of action to recover. What many people do when faced with such a situation is that they choose to keep themselves unaware of their losses; they keep themselves in the dark purposefully, but this can only be a source of more tension and stress. Expose the wounds, bring your losses out into the light. By doing this, you will only have to experience the pricking of your losses at once, no matter how hard it may be. Once you are over the damages, you can start recovering, rather than staying in a constant state of depression and doing nothing to improve your situation.

Be Consistent: No matter the magnitude of the setback that you have experienced, if you let it disturb your resolve, you will only lose more. Neglecting your rules, current budget, and due bill dates can make a financial setback even more challenging to recover. Evaluate your expenses and reset your priorities accordingly so you can free up some extra money. This will make it easier for you to start saving again. Reevaluating your budget and taking active steps will act as a stress reliever and help you deal with the stress and anxiety of the situation. You will certainly feel a lot better by taking action, even if the case doesn't get better for some time.

Take Care of Yourself: The statement, "Money is a tool, not a consequence," is even more valid now. You cannot let your problems get the better of you. Do not let yourself over-stress and lose sleep. Do not indulge in excessive smoking or drinking. Only when you are feeling 100%, both physically and mentally, you can take any steps to improve your situation.

A Satisfied You is a Rich You

This probably would be the best advice you are going to hear from anyone. Yeah, you might have heard it a thousand times before. But have you ever seriously adopted this advice in your practical life? The statements, 'money doesn't bring you happiness, money is temporary' we have all heard them countless times. However, there is only a tiny percentage of people who actually think and act this way.

There is an important link between money and happiness. As they say, rich nations and rich people are way happier than the poorer countries or communities; and this is a fact. However, you must note that the way money affects happiness is not as great as many people may think. If you have food to eat, clothes to wear, and a house to live, having a higher amount of disposable income has only but a small influence on your happiness.

Yes, of course, money brings you happiness, but to what extent? We only know one piece of the puzzle, what about the rest of the story? Studies and real-life experiences have proved that more money can lead your life to be more miserable, let alone make you happy. Here, it is not being implied that you should start living like a monk or become a money hater. The key is balance, not the balance of riches, but the balance of mind. With the right balance of mind, even the poorest of people and as well as the richest of people stay happy.

Chapter 4 – Budgeting

There are two types of people, those who hate rules and the second who love rules. If you are the latter, you will just love the idea of a household budget, and if you are the former, well, you are going to have a hard time falling in love with a budget. The thing is a proper household budget is absolutely necessary for you to manage your money.

When we talk about managing the money that you already have, nothing takes precedence over the budget as it is an essential part of financial management. A budget is a plan on paper that determines the way you are going to save or spend your money. It helps you allocate the desired amounts of money at the beginning of a financial month and will enable you to successfully manage you living within the limits of your monthly income. If you still think the idea of a budget is scary, you are guaranteed to fall face first in love once you try it. Your budget will completely transform the way you experience your monetary affairs, and for the better.

This chapter is all about teaching you how to make a good household budget. Some of you might've even have tried budgeting before, but it just did not work out for you; that is because you didn't have the tips you needed for budget creation. Not only will you learn to make a household budget the professional way, but you will learn to measure the extent of your compliance with the spending spreadsheets.

You must remember, a budget is not just for the hard times. A budget is for all times. When you are a consistent budgeter, you ensure that the good financial times continue for long.

The Importance of a Budget

There are more reasons to keep a budget than you know because it has more to do with your psychology than just recording your income and expenditure. Here are five reasons for the importance of budgeting and why all financial experts recommend it.

Budgeting Keeps You Focused: Budgeting helps you to figure out your goals in the long-term and keeps you consistent in working towards them. If you go living on your life aimlessly, throwing your money away at every little shiny object that catches your eye, how are you ever going to be able to achieve your life goals? When you budget, it forces you to draw out a goal map—saving money, keeping track of your progress, and bringing your dreams to life will be all part of the goal map. Your budget keeps continually reminding you of your long-term goals; so, you keep working to achieve them. Here is how it works: when you see a brand-new shirt or a fantastic pair of shoes you want to buy, you will stop when you realize that it doesn't fit in your budget. It may hurt for a while, but when the budget reminds you that you are saving for the new car, it will be effortless for you to suppress your wish to buy and walk away happily.

Keeps you away from spending the money you do not have: Credit card debt has become ubiquitous today. A massive number of spenders have accumulated credit card debt as they spend money they do not even have, making them sink deeper into debt. In fact, the average credit card debt in the United States was $6,194 in 2019, and this figure only sees an increase every year. 55% percent of Americans who have a credit card, also have credit card debt; this is proof of how widespread and easy spending out of your means is.

Before credit cards, it was easy for consumers to know if they were spending within limits. As a month concluded, they would know they are on track if they had enough left to pay the rent and save some. Today, everyone uses credit cards, and they have no idea whether they are financially sound or not; the only time they know things are going unwell is when they find themselves deep into debt. However, by creating a budget and sticking to it, you will never get yourself in such a vulnerable position. You will exactly be aware of the money to be allocated to your income, expenditure, and savings.

Yeah, adding numbers and writing down in your budget diary is not as fun as a shopping spree. But imagine, you will be boarding the plane off to your vacation in Turks and Caricos rather than making an appointment with a debt counselor next year.

A Happy Retired Life: A budget not only keeps you away from wasting your money and spending in the right way, so you do not incur any debt but also ensures that your savings are on track. If you allocate a part of your monthly income to savings in your budget, you are sure to enjoy this little extra effort in a grand way down the road.

Helps you Identify the Mistakes: Did you have trouble answering the question about the last time when you made a spending mistake? If you were a budgeter, the question would have been answered right away. Establishing a budget enables you to look carefully at your spending patterns. You will notice that you are wasting money on unnecessary things. Do you use up all the data on your costly mobile data plan? Do you really need a new PS4? Budgeting enables you to reassess your money habits and change them according to your goals.

Budgeting Relieves Stress: Sticking to your budget will also enable you to sleep better. Many of us have tossed and turned for many nights fretting about bills and rents. Without a budget, you allow your money to control you. Take the control back, take charge of your life, and feel more at ease.

How to Make A Budget?

There are three main principles for establishing a household budget.

Compare your current monthly expenditure with your current monthly income.

Cut down your spending, so it is within the limits of your income.

Allocate your money for the different purposes adequately.

In the very first chapter, you were told to ask yourself a set of questions. Answering those questions would have gotten you set and ready to make your budget, but even if you have not gathered all that information yet, no worries. We will do it again, and this time, if you want to make the budget, you will want to follow the instructions. It is recommended that you finish reading this chapter before you start making your budget.

Before you start reading and writing, find yourself a reasonable budget template. It is entirely your choice whether you want to budget with pen and paper or with a budget spreadsheet on your computer or smartphone, while the latter is easy and convenient, many people prefer the former method too. You can download a sample budget template online and start adding the data straight away.

Step 1: **Gather every recent financial document you can find.** You want to have as much content on your hands as possible. You want to have every bank statement, salary bill, utility bill, grocery receipt, and all other documents with any information about your income or expenses from the last six months. The key to creating a good budget is to find out the monthly average for income and expenses; hence, the more the information you can find, the more reliable the monthly average you calculate.

Step 2: **Enlist all your sources of income.** If you are self-employed or have multiple sources of income, you should be sure to record all of them. If you have a variable income (if it varies according to the level of business or sales), add a minimum income amount by using your lowest monthly income from last year; it will serve as a baseline income when setting up the budget. If the income is in a regular paycheck form, where there is an automatic deduction of taxes, you can just use the net income as it will serve the purpose. Calculate the average monthly income by adding the sum of all income money in the last six months and averaging it out by dividing it by six.

Step 3: **Enlist all your expenses.** Finding all your payments recorded in documents will not be an easy task. Calculating the exact amount of money, you spend in a month can only be a possibility when you account for each dollar spent and then adding it up at the end of the month. So, what can we do when we don't have all of that data? Surely there are some expenses to the amount of which you already know, so write them down. These can be the house rent, car insurance, your kids' school fees, etc. The amounts that you do not know, you can make an educated prediction by using the past receipts or the idea you have about how much would be spent. You would have to do this for the first month, but afterward, you'll have it all recorded.

Step 4: **Income VS. Expenditure.** If results show that your income is more than your expenses, you are good to go. This also means that you can funnel the excess income to specific areas, for instance, your retirement savings or paying off debt.

Furthermore, if income is more than expenses, you should consider opting for the "50-30-20" budget. In a 50-30-20 budget, 50% of your income should be allocated to your needs or commodities, your wants should be allocated 30%, and 20% of your budget should go to savings or paying off debt. On the contrary, if the expenses are greater than income, you will need to make changes.

Step 5: **Make the required changes.** If you have managed to identify and enlist all your expenses accurately, your ultimate goal should be to have the income and expenses on the same level. When your expenses are more than your income, try to find the areas in your expenses that you can cut back on. Almost all of your variable expenses can be cut back to some extent. As all these expenses are usually non-essential, it is easy to save up a few dollars in each of the areas to move you closer to leveling your income and expenses.

Step 5 marks the last phase of creating the budget. The next thing you need to do is practically implement the plan. After the budget has been set up, monitoring, and recording the amount spent in each expense category is a crucial step, you should do this every day. Use the same spreadsheet you used to create the budget to record all these expenses.

Estimating the amount of cash, you have spent in each category in a month will stop you from overspending and enable you to identify the unnecessary or problematic spending habits. By taking out a few minutes every day to record your expenses, you will make things much more comfortable rather than filing all the expenses of the month at once.

If you are unconfident about this type of budgeting, try using the envelope system. Here, you divide cash for separate categories in separate envelopes and only spend money from one envelope for its particular purpose. When the money runs out of one envelope, you will have to stop spending in that category.

The Best Ways to Deal with a Budget Deficit

A budget deficit is most commonly known in terms of a governmental budget, but the same term can be used to describe a gap in your household budget. Simply put, a household budget deficit is when the sum of your expenses surpasses your income. There can be a variety of reasons behind a budget deficit, but there are two broad categories. Either a decrease in income, such as joblessness, slow business, or an increase in expenses, such as unexpected bills or accidents. Regardless of what may cause a deficiency in your budget, there are budgeting strategies you can adopt to get yourself a budget surplus.

DECREASE EXPENSES

This probably is the most apparent option. When you have more going out than coming in, you must try and lower your spending. Cutting expenses might be relatively tougher if you are in a short-term budget deficit. The reason being that all the significant payments like rent and utility bills are static and will not be changed much in a short time. However, there is a lot of flexibility to reduce expenses in the average budget. You can try cutting food expenses by 20%; this might be tough but not impossible. Furthermore, temporarily stop saving for unnecessary things or non-commodities like vacations or furniture.

To mitigate your budget deficit, eliminate all your planned savings like travel and retirement savings, stick to a stringent budget. Resist all your temptations to buy things that you do not immediately need if you can live without it, try to postpone buying.

INCREASE INCOME

This is the second most obvious way to fill up your budget deficit, although it is not the most straightforward. Virtually all of us can decrease expenses, but not all of us can increase income, especially people who work full-time jobs with fixed paychecks and cannot operate a side hustle. There are a variety of ways to increase our income; we will discuss them in greater detail in the next chapter.

ANTICIPATE THE DEFICIT

If you can predict that a large payment is around the corner, and you may face a budget deficit, you can start taking steps to fill up the gap. It is an excellent idea to start saving up some cash before there is a deficit. For instance, if you know you have a parental leave coming up and you estimate the expenses to exceed your monthly income by $500, you can prepare yourself for the 6-month parental leave by saving up $3000 before you take leave from office.

DON'T LET IT BE CASUAL

Budget deficits are entirely normal, and almost all of us experience them now and then in life. However, if you see that your budget deficit remains a constant factor, whether you are employed or unemployed or not in any extraordinary situation, then you have certainly got a problem. When your expenditure surpasses your income regularly, you can still use the strategies mentioned above; however, you need to take steps at the next level. Rather than merely trying to lower the variable expenses such as grocery money, you also need to reduce the fixed expenses. Find yourself a cheaper apartment or sell your car and use public transport instead. Asking for a raise will not help you handle the long-term budget deficit; you should consider a new job that pays more.

Sticking to The Plan

Adhering to your budget and maintaining consistency is not an easy task at all, although it is the most satisfying one. Sticking to a budget does not necessarily mean that you are going to deprive yourself of all luxuries in life. If you enjoy going on a family dinner every week or getting new movies, you can still continue to do what you like as long as it stays within the limits of how much you can spend.

Even if you have created a well-thought-out budget, and have invested a lot of time, the trickiest part is adhering to your plan. You might want to sneak some dollars away from your vacation savings to get you children a new XBOX game even though you have used up all of the entertainment budget. Your willpower is going to be an essential part, but your heart can be persuasive. Here is how you can manage to stay on track even when you feel weak against your spending desires.

An Accountability Buddy: Teamwork wins the game. As a one-man army, you will find it extremely hard to stick to your plans. It helps a great deal when you have someone on your side when it comes to household budgets. For most of us, our accountability buddy can be our partner. Still, it can be anyone from a family member to an office colleague. As long as you share similar views on money, you are good to go. When you have someone to stop you from violating your budget goals and encourage you when you are low on motivation, following your budget plan because instantly easier.

Get Rid of the Credit Card: Well, not literally, but stop taking your credit card with you when you go shopping. Remember and internalize this; a credit card will never help you stick to your budget plan; it can only distract you. If you want to follow your plan, only use the money you have. Never use money that you don't own, and that's weighed down with hefty interest rates. Instead, only use the money you have, that's cash or debit card.

Be Practical: By setting unrealistic and impractical rules, you do nothing but pave the way for yourself to ultimately violate those rules. It is essential to ascertain that your budget is realistic. First, if you are going to set entirely impossible goals, you will not be able to stick to the plan as soon as you start. Second, if you set a budget that is hard to follow, you're going to deviate at some point. In both cases, you don't stick to the plan, opening the way for more budget violations. Cutting back your grocery expense so much that you get only bread and beans every supper or discarding your entire entertainment budget are examples of impractical budget solutions. Depriving yourself will make you more likely to rebel against the budget. Cut back logically, do not cut out all that you love.

Use the Envelope System: Using envelopes to segregate your money into the different categories is one tremendous way to curb budgeting mistakes. When managing and shuffling the numbers on spreadsheets or budget worksheets, we tend to mix up the numbers often, and it can be a frustrating experience for many people. On the other hand, putting your cash in separate envelopes for each expenditure category is a fantastic way to avoid the fuss of numbers. On top of that, it gives budgeting a physical feel and keeps you away from mindlessly borrowing money from one category to spend in another.

Chapter 5 – Increase Inflow, Decrease Outflow

Now that you've learned to make a budget, you need to stick to it. Whether you are facing a budget deficit, or you want to increase the surplus so you can save more, increasing the inflow and decreasing the outflow of income is a constant job you should be working on. Regardless of your financial situation, you should work on it even when you have a healthy budget surplus; this way, you will ensure that your surplus never turns into a deficit.

This chapter is all about showing you ways to increase the income and cut back on the spending. Although all of the examples mentioned below may not exactly fit into your lifestyle, they can still trigger your mind to come with innovative ways to improve your finances.

Ways to Cut Expenditure

In this section, you will find a treasure box of ideas for shredding off the extra expenses, all organized category-wise. Some of the ideas we have talked about are simple and small but can yield significant profits over time, especially if they are applied along with other economic measures.

Do not discard any of these ideas right away. If implementing one of them seems like a significant change or sacrifice, consider relaxing it down to something more agreeable. You should be accepting of everything; concentrate more on how spending less is going to help you rather than all that you will miss. Sometimes when you feel like you can't give up on a particular thing, you realize you can do just fine when you spend some time without it; even so, you may also recognize that it actually improves your quality of life when you don't have it. For instance, using public transportation rather than your car gives you extra time to think, read, or relax.

AVAIL CHEAP DEALS

Before we address the specific areas of your household expenses, here are a few tips for you to get the maximum out of your money, regardless of what you are spending on. There are several fantastic sites on the internet having a catalogue of all the hottest deals in your vicinity. Whether you are looking for a wedding dress, a new car, a plasma TV or a new fridge, before you go out to buy anything, looking just online for any offers you are sure to find discounts. You must build a habit of looking out for offers when you want to buy something; this will surely save you tons of cash in the long term.

Here is another important piece of advice about advertising: Try always to buy things when they have a discount on them, however, don't buy anything just because it's on sale. Rather than basing your decision to purchase an item on the discount, you should only base your buying decisions on necessity. When you skim through the Sunday magazine in search of deals and discounts, you are tempted to purchase things you do not need. So, do not forget your budget when looking for deals. If you fail to resist a sale, you must address this spending problem. The best way through this problem is to only look for deals when you need to buy something; looking at sales and advertisements when you don't need to buy anything, will only lead you to make spending mistakes.

How to Save On Groceries?

The average person spends about $250 a month on groceries. An average couple spends nearly double the amount. When we talk about the monthly grocery expenditure for a family of four, the amount can go up to a whopping $1200 a month! That is a fortune. In this piece, you will read some tips that can help you bring your grocery costs by 20%.

Change Your Meals

Simple is good. If you think of your dinner as a healthy feast of chicken and meat with French bread and salad, plus a chocolate cake as dessert, you need to change your perception of a good meal. Health, nutrition and good taste do not necessarily mean buying expensive groceries. Here is a list of groceries that will help you cut the cost but maintain the same nutrition and taste.

Oatmeal	Cereal
Cream of Wheat	Bananas
Eggs	Apple
Bread	Beans

King Ari Dane

Lentils
Rice
Pasta
Potatoes
Sweet potatoes
Carrots
Canned Tomatoes
Squash
Zucchini
Onions
Broccoli
Salsa
Chicken
Green Salad
Spinach
Ground Turkey
Peanut Butter

Keep an Account as you Shop

When you're at the grocery store and moving through the aisles as you're picking stuff up, get the phone out of your pocket and open the calculator app. Keep adding the prices of all the products that you pick up, and this will help you keep inside the budget range and also keep you from buying unnecessary stuff. On top of that, it will save you from the fuss of having things removed from your bill as the cashier makes your receipt.

Round-Up All the Prices

When you put something in your shopping cart and add its price on the calculator, try to round the cost to the nearest upper 50 cents. For instance, if something costs $2.6, add $3, round $25.2 to $25.5. This way, you will stay under the budget boundary, and you will thank yourself when you will have an extra ten bucks left as you check out.

Exploit What You Have

There is always something somewhere you can use and cook up a meal. Raid your pantry and look for different and innovative meals you can come up with the ingredients you have. You do not have to go to the supermarket when you already have a couple of lamb ribs and canned beans in your fridge. Utilize everything you have in every way possible. There is a variety of ways you can get more out of all types of foods.

Think Before You Bulk Buy

Buying your groceries in bulk can automatically seem like a cheap option. But before you dive in, think about which waters are better to dive in to. Do not automatically assume that buying in large quantities at discount stores is cheaper. When you are on a budget, make certain to stop for a moment and compare the prices per unit for what you are buying. It is really tempting to stock up, but you really don't need to buy more than you require. Buying cereal in bulk might be a good option when you have children, but if it is just you and your partner, a 40-unit box of yoghurt will only lead to a loss.

Frozen Food is your New Best Friend

Say hi to freezer meals! There are countless freezer meals recipes you can find on the internet. Set aside a weekend to prepare a bunch of frozen meals and set yourself tension-free for a week. Preparing once means you can utilize the bulk-buying strategy and preserve the pre-cooked food in freezers. Not only does this save you money, but it also saves you time.

Ignore the Eye-level Products

Grocery stores place the more expensive or good-looking products in the aisles so that they are on the same level as your line of sight as you walk down a corridor. The next time you go shopping, notice how the expensive items on the shelves lie right in front of your eyes? It is done on purpose, don't let the grocers steal your resolve. Do not fall for marketing tricks like these, instead, look up or down on the shelves and buy the cheaper alternatives. Remember this trick the next time you go shopping, better yet, write it down on the grocery list you have just made.

Do not Go Shopping Hungry

Hunger makes us forget ourselves, and that is true in every context! A lot of people make a lot of silly mistakes when they are hungry. They tend to say things they do not mean, get angry quickly, and pick up everything that brings water to their mouth as they stroll down the grocery store aisles. You might get away with other things you might have done when you were in the hunger-rage, your grocery bill will not spare you easily. Go shopping with a satisfied stomach, and make sure you only buy what you should.

How to Save on Transportation?

After the housing costs, your transportation costs might be second on your list of largest expenditure categories. You might already know of some ways like taking the bus to work or cycling; there are other less commonly known tricks you can use to bring your transportation bill down.

Weight Deduction!

This simple law of physics can save you hundreds of dollars over the years. The extra weight in your car is making it harder for your vehicle to drive more in a given fuel quantity. You can quickly reduce your car's weight up to 100 pounds, and this can improve the fuel economy by 3%.

A Well-maintained Car Saves Money.

Getting your ride regularly tuned can improve the mileage by 4%. Keeping the optimum air pressure in the tires can also improve mileage by the same percentage. So, both these aspects of the car when taken care of simultaneously will enhance your car's mileage by a tremendous 8%!

Be Your Mechanic

Learn to change your own engine oil, and to do simple car repairs. You can get classes from a community college or a skills training program in your area. Better yet, you can just watch tutorials on YouTube. You can learn all sorts of repairs from tuning your car to replacing brake pads.

Drive Economically

You can save a lot of money bringing some changes in your driving. First of all, drive safely. Keeping within speed limits and cautious driving will keep you away from repair costs and traffic violation fines. Secondly, keep the RPM below three as you drive. Do not step on the gas in the first two gears, or when the car starts to move. Always try to gain speed gradually. Use the brakes as sparingly as possible; when you see a red light coming up, there is no use keeping your foot on the accelerator and then braking abruptly at the signal. Let your vehicle slow down on itself. This will preserve your brakes and save fuel.

Get Yourself a Bike

A bicycle is an excellent investment. Rather than starting your car when you are heading to town to get some bread, get on your bike instead, save money and exercise.

Buy Your Airline Tickets On Time

You would already be aware of the fact that booking your flight on the eleventh hour can cost you a fortune. Furthermore, when you are booking your flight a week or two before, consider buying on a Monday or Tuesday. The first two days of the week will typically offer the cheapest ticket rates as compared to the rest of the week.

Carpool

If you share a ride to work, you can lower travel costs and your carbon footprint. Several technological tools are making carpooling ever more accessible, even for employees who work with small companies. There are a handful of sites that enable you to share your ride to work with employees who work in the same area as you.

How to Save on Clothing?

The average American spends approximately $1700 on clothes and accessories annually. If you want to manage your money, you certainly do not want to be spending this much on just clothes. Here is how you can save on clothing without sacrificing the quality of the garments you wear.

Buy Socks in Bulk

Although buying socks in bulk means you'll have to wear the same color every day, a timeless black for men or the stock skin color socks for women when bought in bulk will save you money.

Shop at the End of the Season

Buy now for next year. With some planning and forethought, buy clothes for the upcoming winter in the spring clearance sale. Although you won't be able to wear them right away, you can enjoy the perks of your timely shopping next year, and with a great deal of savings.

Exchange Clothes with Pals

When a season starts, you and your friends can go through your wardrobes and trade items you won't wear. Set a trading day with your friends or family and sell any clothes you still left with. Make money and get new clothes!

Avoiding Unnecessary Expenses

Avoiding unnecessary expenditure might seem difficult at first, but all it requires is a bit of consistency. Here are a few tips that will help you avoid unnecessary spending.

1. Don't waste your money on guarantees

Ask yourself if the guarantees sold separately are really worth the expense. Indeed, some of these guarantees are not worth the cost, so be alert, especially in the field of electronics.

As soon as you buy an electronic device such as a television, headphones or a computer, we are offered an extended warranty. The problem is that the price to purchase this guarantee sometimes represents up to 1/3 of the cost of the object, which is clearly too high!

Ask before spending on an extended warranty because most devices already have a warranty from the manufacturer.

2. Lotto tickets, an UNNECESSARY expense to avoid

Do you have the bad habit of spending on one or more lotto tickets every week?

Knowing the minimal chances that you have of winning a significant amount of money in the Lotto, this expenditure is entirely useless. The lotto should, therefore, be avoided if you want to save money every week!

The chances of winning are so minimal in the lottery that there is no reason for you to put down your money like this!

3. Don't buy the latest phone model!

Are you one of those people who like to regularly upgrade their electronic devices or phones as soon as a new model arrives on the shelves?

Since they release new models every year (both for game consoles and phones, for example), you may be tempted to change to the brand-new model!

It is an unnecessary expense that you should definitely avoid considering the minimal changes that are made to most devices. In most cases, it is usually an upgrade to the camera. Control yourself and keep your phone for another year to save money.

4. Slot machines are a no-no!

Slot machines in some establishments and even online can make you lose a lot of money! In fact, everything related to casinos will make you lose money, a lot of money! The house always wins, and you would do well to remember this. They are rigged up to make you think that you have a chance, but you don't.

5. The coffee from the restaurant you order every day!

Instead of spending between 3 and 5 dollars per day for a simple coffee, make your own coffee at home and buy a thermos to bring your coffee with you.

A little tip that easily saves 10 to 20 dollars every week and even more for some people.

6. The newspaper - another unnecessary expense

Papers end up being expensive! If we calculate the amount spent, for example, over a full year, it can represent a lot of money.

You have the internet at home and work, so why spend more on the newspaper? Just read the news on your phone or tablet, it is simple!

7. Cigarettes - an expense to avoid!

Cigarettes do your body no good. They don't just hurt your lungs; they also cause a deep hole in your wallet. The government has levied a bunch of taxes on cigarettes, so there is no need to spend this much on them. It is just a bad habit, and you should let it go.

In addition to being very unhealthy, cigarettes are costly. If you are a smoker, it is undoubtedly the most useless expense to eliminate, and this, as quickly as possible.

8. The landline phone

Do you pay for a mobile plan? Many people have a mobile phone, so why keep paying for the home phone every month?

A fixed line package can cost more than 20 dollars depending on the options, so imagine how much you will save by cancelling this monthly package?

9. Stop spending on restaurants!

For those who work outside the home, the temptation to eat in a restaurant with work colleagues can be strong, isn't it? It is costly to eat every day at the restaurant or even once every week. Better to make your lunch in the morning when you get out of bed and save a lot of money each week!

10. Cut into parking lots

Parking lots end up being awfully expensive! It is better to evaluate your options; being a bicycle or public transportation; Metro, bus, parking meters, trains, there is no shortage of choices. It is essential to calculate carefully to be sure that this does not equal the same price or even more!

Ways to Bulk Income

Slashing your expenditure by using thrifty tips and tricks and avoiding unnecessary expenses is only one half of the puzzle. The second part, however, is to increase your income. When both the inflow of cash is increased, and the outflow is decreased simultaneously, you can move closer to your milestones at muzzle velocity.

In this chapter, we will go through unique ways to bulk your income you might have never heard before. On top of that, we are going to emphasize how you can use the money you already have in ways to increase your wealth. Talk about earning money with money.

What to Do When You Need Cash ASAP?

You can get cash by redeeming your recycled material: This is not only going to help you overcome a difficult financial problem but is an environmentally friendly option too. Recycling centers near you will pay you for every plastic bottle or aluminum can that you bring to recycle. Apart from bottles and cans, you can sell the old computer parts or scrap metal and sell it at recycling rates. Although this solution is not going to be enough for overcoming your problem (unless you gather tons of bottles), the money you will accumulate can be added to the capital from other means, and this is how you will be to put two and two together.

Gather cash by having a garage sale: A garage sale is where you put your old and unused things up for sale; this a way of getting money where you just have to put the items you want to sell out in your front yard and display a garage sale sign along with it. You will get customers pouring soon because everyone is interested in buying things that they need at low prices and not having to buy brand new one. The amount of cash that you're going to raise from your garage sale depends on how many things you have sold, as this is not an instant solution, selling out all your items may even take a week, so that is something to be considered. You may be able to raise a few hundred by selling things you don't need, not only will this give you money, it is the best solution for clearing up your home of unwanted stuff.

Ask your friends or family to help you out: A friend in need is a friend indeed, and whenever you are in a problem, it is always best to consult the people close to you, unless you need to keep something private. It is one of the intrinsic properties of your relationship with your friends and family that they are going to help you when you need it and vice versa. Even when they do not have any money to offer you, they can still give you the mental support and their precious advice. While one person will not be able to lend you money that would suffice, if you can get 2 or 3 people to pay you, you will have a considerable amount on your hands. When those people have such a problem, you could return the favor.

Ask your boss for a new paycheck: When you are in a situation where you need money immediately. You think getting a higher pay now will solve your woes. Surely you could request your boss for increasing and rolling out your payment early and if your boss is considerate and is facing no problems in giving you the salary, this going to be fantastic for you as you won't have to ask people or sell your property.

Earn More at Your Job

If you are a public office holder or privately employed, but law inhibits you from running a business or have an additional source of income, the employer you currently work for may provide the only immediate source of extra income.

If you work at an hourly wage, let your employer know that you are willing to work overtime. This option would be even better if the demand for your company's product or service is increasing. If the company is opening a new store or office, you can add an extra shift to your day, work more every day, or also work on weekends.

Requesting for a salary raise is another option, but for this, you need to justify your request properly. For instance, a raise may be justified if you haven't received one recently, if you have been assigned an additional responsibility without due compensation, or if you have completed an important project successfully. You would be better able to judge whether you deserve a raise or not; even when you don't, there's no harm in trying!

One more way to earn more at your job is by getting a promotion. Inform your boss about your willingness to work at a higher-paying portfolio in the same department. If you have the right qualifications to work in another department, get an appointment with managers of other departments and you can inform them about your interest.

Consider Freelancing!

Freelancing is all the rage in this era. People have started switching from traditional full-time jobs to freelance work. While you will be seeking additional income, you can consider it as a side hustle. Freelancing, in essence, is when you are a free agent, and you can willingly take up any jobs on a contract basis. There are a bunch of freelancing websites on the internet, such as Upwork and Fiverr.

Choose your specialization. As a freelancer, you can get all types of jobs from graphic designing, illustrations, writing, transcriptions, business proposals and the list goes on. Virtually, you can work any tasks that can be shared over the internet. When you sign up, you can choose the fields you specialize in and make a freelancer account.

Initially, you will have a hard time scoring any jobs, because clients are always looking for more experienced professionals. But as soon as you manage to get your first job, it opens the door for new gigs. The dilemma you may face as a freelancer is that at times, you may have no work at all, or you will have more work than you can manage. This may imply an irregular stream of income. Still, as you come into the field of work, you will learn ways to manage your gigs so you can work continually but also without any stress.

Make Money With The Money You Have

There is a common saying, "Make your money work for you." But how exactly? Well, there are different ways to earn money by using the money you already have, but here is the catch, you can only earn enough money when you have enough money. If you are already tight on cash, you will not be able to apply the following ways, but still, you can read for now and practice later when you have the right circumstances.

A High-Yield Savings Account

A high-yield savings account is a category of savings accounts that typically pays you up to 25 times the usual national average of saving account rates. ☐Previously, people opened their savings accounts in the same banks as they had their current accounts in, to make the transfer process seamless between the two accounts.

However, now with the entry of internet-only banks, plus traditional banks also have initiated online bank account opening services. This increase in competition has led the saving account rates to shoot, introducing a new type of savings account with the highest rates, called High-yield savings accounts.

Given the contrast between the rates of high-yield savings account and typical savings accounts, the earnings on the high-yield accounts are significantly higher. For instance, the national average rate on an ordinary savings accounts is a mere 0.10%; so, if you have $5000 in that account, you'd only earn $5 over a year. On the other hand, if you had put the same $5,000 in a high-yield savings account, with a 2% return rate, you would earn $100 over the same period.

If you are looking to open a high-yield savings account, prioritize the online banks because online banks typically offer the highest rates. Furthermore, money transfers are convenient between current accounts and these savings accounts even if the two are held at different financial institutions. Here is a list of important considerations you must make when opening your high-yield savings account:

Interest rate: This factor should be the most significant determinant of your account choice. Is it the rate standard or an initial promotional rate? These account rates are typically elastic and can be changed. However, some banks will indicate that the current advertised rate is only available for the introductory period.

Required initial deposit: There is a specific minimum amount necessary to be deposited when you open a savings account. Compare this amount among the candidate banks and decide which amount will you be comfortable paying.

Minimum balance required: What is the amount of money are you expected to keep in the savings account generally? Choose the minimum balance requirement that you will feel comfortable with because falling below it may make you pay a fee or overturn the interest rate you have been expecting.

Fees: Does the bank charge any fees on this account and how much is it? If it does, how can you avoid it? For instance, by always keeping above the limit and withdrawing only when you should.

Accessing your money: What are the additional options you have for withdrawing your money? Does the bank offer the use of an ATM card or online payments?

Deposit options: What are all the ways the bank offers to deposit money into the account? Can you physically deposit checks at any of the branches, does the bank operate a smartphone application that lets you deposit from mobile? If not so, can you mail the checks in or deposit money using an ATM?

Compounding method: Banks can specify that interest will be compounded on what periods? Will it be compounded daily, monthly, quarterly, semiannually, or annually? An account with a frequent compounding method will increase your yield theoretically.

A high-yield account is no get-rich-quick way. However, it will contribute to your passive income if you have a significant amount deposited in your savings.

Other Ways to Passive Income

Rental Income: The property you own is the money you have in one form. You can lend this money to someone and earn from it. If you own an empty house, apartment or shop, rent it away and make money while you sleep. If you have a room or floor in your home that is sparingly used, you can also rent it to an individual or a family. You can also rent your car; sign a car rental agreement with the person you want to rent it to, and boom you are earning!

Dividend Stocks: Shareholders in public companies with stocks that yield dividends receive payments at regular intervals. The companies pay the dividends after each quarter out of the profits they have earned from the business; the only role you need to play is to buy the stock. The share of the stock determines the dividend you receive, hence, the more the shares you buy, the higher the dividend you receive.

The stocks that you own provide you with income without any activity other than the initial financial investment. These dividend-yielding stocks can be one of the best sources of passive income, although it does include a risk factor. Because the dividend you receive is only a meagre percentage of the total profit earned by the company, you need to have invested quite an amount in the right company's stock to make a healthy amount.

Choosing the right stock and buying and selling at the right time is the key to stock trading. Experts state that too many rookies throw their money at stocks expecting to earn money, but they only end up losing. When you choose a company, select the right dividend share. For instance, the dividend per share offered by Coca Cola on its stock was 2.9% in 2019, so of all the profit earned, Coca Cola gives 2.9% of the increase in the price of a stock to its owner. This may not seem like a very good investment upfront, but stocks like Coca Colas are for long-term investment. You buy them now and sell them down the road over months or years; you can make the decision to sell your stock when you anticipate that a particular company is going to suffer a loss in the future and you can invest somewhere else.

Chapter 6 – The Credit Score

We have already discussed what credit reports and credit scores are and how you can access them in chapter 1. It's tricky to navigate bad credit in the contemporary world. Several firms use your credentials to determine whether to do business or trading with you and negotiate prices for the goods and services you use. So before moving ahead, you need to understand the idea of credit repair.

Credit repair is repairing the poor credit rating that may have escalated for numerous reasons. Repairing credit status can be as straightforward as disputing details about errors with credit agencies. Identity theft and the damage it causes may require some extra credit repair work. Another important aspect of credit repair is to work with critical financial problems, such as financial management, and addressing legitimate borrowers' concerns.

Usually, we equate credit repair with those with poor credit. The reality is that at some point in their lifetime, sometimes even more than once, everybody needs to engage in credit repair. Of course, those with poor credit scores typically need it the most. So, also when you've got an average or decent ranking, you might want to raise it much more, either to increase your chances of being accepted and eligible for some loan or to get lower costs and favorable terms.

Credit repair includes two factors that we need to focus on. These factors are:

Eradicating or minimizing the unfavorable entries:

The process begins by getting a copy of your new credit report, then checking every line item. If any lines display negative or damaging information, those are the ones that you want to focus on. The first objective in examining the negatives is to inspect for anything that may be in error or fault. These may involve collections that are not associated with you, records or accounts with unfavorable payment history belonging to someone else, including an ex-spouse, or open balances that you have compensated for a long time.

So, did you know that excessive credit utilization has some serious drawbacks that can weigh down your credit score? Excessive credit usage has been one of the most significant potential disadvantages, and one that is ambiguous and vague to most customers. Excessive credit usage is calculated by what is known as the percentage or ratio of credit usage. That is the total amount that you owe on your lines of credit, split by your overall credit limits.

Okay so let us assume you have four credit cards with a $15,000 cumulative credit limit. If you owe over the four cards a minimum of $11,250, the credit utilization level is 75%. This utilization rate of 75% of the credit will be considered excessive and therefore, will drag down your credit score. Credit use is the second largest decisive factor in credit score, except for the history of payment. It contributes to about 30% of your ranking, so it is a critical mission to keep that amount at a manageable level.

Increase positive entries:

The increase in positive credit entries is equally essential. Often a lack of quality credit weighs down a credit score. An absence of adequate credit can even hold it back. If you want a fantastic credit score, you will, of course, want to make the payments on time. Yet paying off a debt or a credit card is one of the easiest ways to boost your credit score. Moreover, you can also get extra points and increase the positive entries by paying off credit cards or an instalment loan.

So, if you have you have poor credit, you will undoubtedly have to work to eliminate as many negative items as feasible.

Now, the reality and solution to credit repair should be quite clear. Credit repair requires correcting a bad credit rating, whether it is as easy as reporting errors or fixing certain factors due to which the evaluation might have dropped in the first place.

The Importance of a Good Credit Score

The answer is clear to how you got bad credit: the history of the payments you make and acquired loans tell the lender it is not safe to lend to you. Bad credit typically implies that you have been unsuccessful in the past to make payments on time as defined on your credit contracts. The credit report also considers any other public records such as your citizenship, tax records, and legal rulings against you. Hence, not having a clean legal record and failing to show accountability in your payments deteriorates your credit.

There also can be other reason such as declaring bankruptcy, paying only the least amount every time and identity theft. Having declared bankruptcy in the past severely damages your credit report. Paying the lowest amount each time you make a payment to will also worsen your credit score. If you pay less, this means you will be paying off debt for longer and hence, you will pay more money in the form of interest. Even if you make your payments on time and pay more than the lowest amount, you can still get bad credit if someone else uses your credit card and makes big purchases and runs up giant bills that you cannot pay.

These are only some of the ways your credit rating is harmfully impacted, and by avoiding these, you can have better credit. Recover your credit score by paying on time, reducing your debt by paying off loans, not maxing out on your card and by keeping an eye on your credit score.

Here's why lenders do not want to loan to people with bad credit; someone with bad credit is an evident risk for moneylenders. When you apply for a loan, other people also apply alongside you, and this means competition. If you have an inferior credit score than another applicant, there is very little reason for a creditor to loan out to you (a higher-risk option) and not to someone with a better credit score (a low-risk option).

After having read this piece, you might have realized the significance of having good credit. Regardless of if you want to take a loan, a good credit score holds great importance for other things such as getting a house on rent, landing a job and getting loans at low interest rates.

Improving Credit

Boosting your credit score will assist you in qualifying for lower interest rates and better terms; this also helps you to borrow money for personal purposes (a car loan, a home equity loan, a credit card, etc.) or you can purchase products, rent a property, etc. to launch or expand a business.

Credit repair is not complicated. It won't take you several months to boost your credit score. To rebuild your credit and raise your credit score, continue to follow these certain secrets — and increase your ability to invest money on terms you can manage and afford.

Do you know the secret to increase your credit score? Do you think your credit score could be a little bit better? You have already seen a large number of people on the internet talking about just how with the tremendous success they went through the same thing. So, what exactly did they implement? Do they have any magic? Or some secret tricks that you do not have? Well, yes, this might be the truth. Maybe they know these fantastic tricks, and now you will know them too!

Make micropayments: What you need to do is to make small payments throughout the month. Micropayments will lower your credit card's balance. You can even view your credit card as a debit card, paying electronically when an order is released. Making multiple payments over the month acts on a credit indicator called credit utilization which has a powerful impact on ratings and scores. If you can keep your usage low rather than allowing it to rise towards a payment due date, your score will gain automatically.

Try A higher credit limits: Did you know if your credit card limit rises and the balance remains the same, it will automatically lower the total use of credit? So, in such a scenario what you need to do is to contact the credit card company to inquire if you can get a higher limit without a "hard" credit inquiry, which can potentially drop a few points in your score.

Dispute incorrect late-payment entries and credit report errors: Mistakes occur. Your mortgage lender could record a late payment which was eventually paid on time. A credit card provider can fail to register a payment correctly. You can dispute incorrect late-payment entries whether in existing or expired accounts, the very same way you question derogatory tags. Another element weighing heavily on your credit score is your payment background and history, so try hard to fix those errors.

Become an authorized user: Find a family member or friend who has a long and responsible record of using a credit card. Ask them to add you to their credit card as an authorized user. The account owner does not have to allow you to use the card or make any transaction for your benefits.

Decide and play the game: Okay, so let us assume that an account went to collection, you never paid or compensated it, and due to this, the collection agency decided to give up. Now all that is in your hand is the reference and entry to your credit report. In such a scenario, you can still challenge the entry. Many people do. And sometimes such issues and entries are resolved.

When you dispute the error, the credit bureau tells the agency to verify the claims and information. A few agencies will. Others do not want to, especially collection agencies. They will completely ignore the order, and in such cases, they are required to resolve the matter and remove the entry from your credit report.

What this suggests is that the smaller firms, such as collection agencies or retail borrowers or small to medium-sized providers, are much less likely to react to the credit bureaus. They don't need a headache. Banks, credit-card firms, auto finance firms, and mortgage companies are more inclined to respond. But if you want — you do not necessarily have to use this technique; we are just suggesting that some people make decisions to use this technique — you can dispute information in the assumption that the creditor won't respond or reply. (This is the tactic that credit repair companies use to improve the ratings of their clients.) If the creditor refuses to answer, the entry is deleted.

Keep credit cards open: If you are trying to boost your credit profile, you should be aware that shutting down credit cards will make the job more challenging. Closing a credit card makes you lose the credit limit of that card when determining the total credit usage, which can result in a lower score. Leave the card open and periodically use it so that the provider will not lock it.

Can you improve your credit by 100?

So, if you are dealing with a lower score, you're better placed than anyone with a solid credit history to make gains. Now, what do you think? Is a 100-point increase realistic?

Did you know that the lower a person's score, the more often a 100-point increase is accomplished? That is because there is a lot of upsides and minor changes that will lead to a higher score.

And if you begin with a higher score, you probably do not need 100 maximum points to make a significant difference with the credit products that you will get. Simply, polishing your credit will make life so much easier and give you the best chance to compete for the right terms on credit cards or mortgages.

Chapter 7 – A Guide to Managing Household Finances

The Money Saver House

If you want to save money at home, you need to make sure that you decorate your home and plan your life in such a way that you can save as much as possible. Remember, a significant amount of your money is going to be spent on your home upkeep and yourself. Therefore, by creating a "money-saver" house, you can eventually save up quite a bit. Here are some basic things that you can do around the house to save money.

Do not waste electricity

It is something fundamental, and they have told us a thousand times, but we still do it. Do not leave the electrical devices on when you are not using them and do not leave them on standby since they continue to use energy. Although it will not take your bill overboard, it still can contribute as much as 12% to your monthly utility bills, and that is a lot.

Efficient bulbs

In line with the above, if you are not in a room, why leave the light on? Turn it off whenever you are not using it. Besides, we recommend replacing all house light bulbs with low-energy ones, they are more expensive, but in the long run, you will save a lot of money. And if you can buy LEDs, even better since they are even more efficient.

To give you an idea, efficient bulbs consume up to 80% less energy than incandescent bulbs and have up to 10 to 15 times longer service life.

Do not waste water

Another thing that you might have been taught since you were a kid but that we keep forgetting from time to time is wastage of water. Turn off the water tap when you are not using it, for example, when you are brushing your teeth, shaving, or soaping the body. About 10 liters of water is wasted in a single minute!

A rather exciting option to save water is to install flow limiters at the tap mouth (aerators), which prevent it from opening beyond a certain angle. Thus, the water consumption of the taps goes from 15 to 8 liters per minute, and that of the shower from 20 to 10 liters.

Coldwater instead of hot

Hot water represents a quarter of the energy consumption of an average home. Therefore, any improvement in this regard will help you reduce the bill substantially. The best are the single-handle taps that allow you to mix hot and cold water and use cold water whenever possible (it is also much healthier for the skin). Also, check the water consumption of your washing machine and dishwasher.

Don't abuse heating and air conditioning

The ideal temperature for the house is around 20°C. For each additional grade, the expense increases between 5% and 10%. At night or when you are not at home, it is best to set it to around 15°C instead of removing it (remember that with digital thermostats, you will control the temperature much better). In winter, try not to cover the radiators or be at home dressed as if it were summer; it is better to have to cover yourself with a blanket than to waste money on heating. And the same can be said in the summer with air conditioning; it is a matter of being at a comfortable temperature, not as if we were stuck in a refrigerator.

Good windows are an investment for the future.

Linking to the topic of heating and air conditioning, many homes are forced to abuse it, due to the loss of energy (heat or cold) that occurs through their windows. For this reason, perhaps the time has come to consider replacing your old and inefficient windows (probably aluminum sliding doors without thermal bridge breakage) for good PVC windows, which prevent your money and the degrees of temperature from escaping so quickly. The best opening system to guarantee good insulation is the folding system. No kidding: with good windows, the energy losses that occur through the window can be reduced by up to 70%.

Installing good windows cannot be considered an expense as such, but rather an investment in the medium-long term since thanks to them, you will save a lot of money on our energy bill and gain in comfort and well-being.

Blinds also count (and a lot)

Of course, good windows must be accompanied by blinds that are at the right height. If we put insulating windows, but the shades are not, we will have thrown the money away, since air will enter through the blinds, ruining the insulation achieved by the windows. However, if you choose a quality shutter, for example, the KÖMMERLING RolaPlus system, you will even improve the overall performance. Therefore, if you have decided to change your windows, we recommend that you also change the blinds.

Efficient appliances

If you must renew any appliance, bet on the most efficient: note that it says Class A on its label and, the more crossings, the better. The best ones are the A +++ (known as Triple-A). Although they are more expensive than those of lower categories, throughout their lives, they will allow you to save more than $500 in electricity.

Perhaps right now you might not have to change any appliance, but what you can do is always use them efficiently and rationally, without wasting energy. For example, do not leave the oven preheating more than necessary or continually open and close the door, or take advantage of the residual heat from the ceramic hob or the iron after turning it off or, as we said when talking about water, use the washing machine and dishwasher only when you can put them at full load.

Be careful with the appliances that consume the most energy

If all the appliances have to be used efficiently, even more so, the ones that consume the most, the refrigerator is by far the one that requires the most energy. So, it is important that it is located in a cool and ventilated place away from heat sources. Also, the fewer times you open it, the better, since each time you do, 7% of energy is lost. Other useful tips to save are not to put hot food in it or keep it full all the time, but with enough space, for air to circulate. Ah! And then you have the microwave, using it instead of the oven, saves between 60 and 70% of energy, as well as a lot of time. The dryer is another of the most energy-consuming appliances. Therefore, use it as little as possible, only when you cannot hang clothes or are in a hurry to have clothes dry.

Check the facilities

The review of the facilities (gas, electricity, etc.) is necessary both for security reasons and to avoid excessive expenses. In new houses, the review should be done every ten years, while those older than 25 years should be done every five years. We recommend that you, first, compare budgets and always go to accredited professionals and companies, thus avoiding unpleasant surprises.

Use your checking account for your current transactions

Your checking account must be your primary bank account used to pay for so-called "current" expenses. If you do not maintain your deposit account with a credit balance, then you will have to pay the interest, any additional fees, and often face payment rejections! Conversely, if you have a comfortable advance, do not use your checking account either to let this money sleep. Your account must have the necessary sums for your expenses; the surplus amount should be transferred to a savings account.

Put your savings in a dedicated account

Opening a savings account is also an important step, probably the most crucial one for your future. It is important to build up cash to be able to finance projects, but also react in the event of the unexpected.

How To Manage Your Money That You Already Have

Do not think that your modest income prevents you from saving? Even a savings of ten dollars, with the interest which remains on the account at the end of the month, makes it possible to create a small nest egg that will grow over time. It's slow, but over time, it always works.

Choosing the Right Mortgage Plan

Investing in property, such as your home, is probably going to be one of the biggest moments of your life, and it can be quite exciting, yet stressful, which is why clients should meet with a financial advisor (or an asset management specialist) to make sure they understand all the terms of the mortgage contract and choose what suits them. The flexibility offered by prepayment, biweekly, and mortgage options can help clients save thousands of dollars in interest and long-term fees.

1. Know how much you can borrow.

By establishing a comprehensive strategy with an advisor, you will make sure you make an informed decision, and you will eliminate some of the stress. Also find out what you can afford. Most banks offer online tools to calculate how much you can borrow.

2. Understand your options.

The characteristics of the loan and your flexibility are just as important as the rate. Many buyers only see this one and the repayment schedule, but there are other things you need to consider, like the prepayment schedule. Can you make one or two additional payments during the year? Some products do not allow this, while prepayment can take years off mortgage payments.

3. Can you transfer your loan?

Some people, especially first-time buyers, change homes after one or two years because they want something bigger, smaller, or just want to move. The possibility of transferring your loan to your new property is, therefore, a key point of the discussion.

4. Before making an offer, get pre-approved.

Although it is useful to have an idea of the loan to which you would be entitled, we strongly recommend that you obtain a pre-approval before setting out in search of a home. So, you will know what is within your reach.

5. Surround yourself with a good team.

For most of us, housing will be the biggest purchase of our lives. Therefore, make sure you make the right decisions by hiring professionals, starting with your advisor, find out how much you can afford to pay and how to structure your loan agreement. Also, find an excellent real estate service provider who understands your needs and who can offer you all essential services, such as an inspector, appraiser, home staging, and notary.

When you get out in the market to look for a mortgage plan, consider the following things:

Compare and choose

Do not stick with the first option you find. Compare the different types of credits, interest rates, and insurance (unemployment and life) that they offer you. Also, consider the response time for credit authorization, as there is a possibility that you may not be suitable for all financial institutions.

Consider other expenses

Like the TAC (Total Annual Cost), and the interest rate! The TAC is a calculation that includes the expenses derived from the financing of this type: commission, insurance, additional charges, etc. On the other hand, the interest rate can be fixed or variable. You need to choose the best interest rate. A fixed rate ensures (regardless of the term) that the interest you pay for five or 30 years will always be the same.

Way to pay

You must choose between fiat currency, times a minimum wage, or Investment Units. These units are necessary for the collection of your mortgage, and each one directly affects the credit you choose. We recommend financing in your local currency since, in this way, you will always know precisely what the amount of your debt is.

Consider that, like an income, the amount of your mortgage should not exceed 30% of your monthly income. Once these elements are chosen, it is time to sign the credit for which you have decided.

After signing

We recommend you carefully read your contract and verify that it complies with what they have offered you. Timely payment of the mortgage will prevent you from incurring late interest. Check if your contract allows you to make advance payments and if yes, it is recommended that you do advance payments when possible. So, you can reduce the time you can pay off your debt and, therefore, you will pay less interest.

Once these points are reviewed, you will be ready to start paying for your property. Remember that it is always best to receive personalized advice. If you have doubts, it is better to visit the websites of the banks before you visit the institution.

The Right Medical Insurance Plan for Your Family

Purchasing the right medical insurance plan could do wonders for your family. Protecting yourself and your family in times of a medical emergency is critical, and it is only doable if you have the right coverage. Otherwise, all the money that you might have saved up in the past few years will go down the drain.

However, with so many insurance plans available in the market, how do you choose the right one? If you want to save money, it's equally important for you to find the best medical insurance plan for your family. Here are a few tips that will help.

The demand for insurance policies is on the rise as more and more people are now looking for health insurance for their family as a guarantee of internal peace in the face of any health problem that their loved ones may have. Choosing the most appropriate policy in each case requires taking into account various factors, both financially and in terms of coverage.

The Fundamental Information

If you want to purchase family health insurance, start by collecting as much information as possible about all the products on the market. Comparing prices and basic coverage is the first step in choosing the insurance that best suits your needs.

Centers and Medical Chart

Knowing the professionals who can assist you is another factor to consider before taking out insurance. In this way, you will be able to assess the proximity of clinics and medical centers, as well as the possibility of continuing to see the doctors you already know.

Copayments

Not all insurers offer them, but some policies determine a payment based on the number of times the service is used, in addition to a lower monthly fee. Assess what best fits your healthcare needs.

International Assistance

Keep in mind that family health insurance must cover all the people who make up the family. If any of you travel regularly, it is important that the policy has national and international coverage to guarantee assistance outside your city and country of residence.

Dental Coverage

Health insurances tend to offer a series of free basic dental services, and the rest subsidize them in part. Find out about the exact conditions since dental care is one of the most requested and most expensive on the market.

Over 60 Years

If there are older people in your family, keep in mind that their medical needs are different. Be sure to choose insurance that guarantees adequate health coverage.

Other Coverage

Services psychology, birth, and family planning should also be considered as hedges of quality health insurance. Knowing their scope and the professionals who lend them is an important factor when contracting a policy.

These are some simple tips that you should keep in mind if you are on the lookout for a comprehensive family insurance policy.

Using Technology to Save Money

The evolution of society has contributed to events on a world scale that are much closer to our hearts. We are acquiring a new vision of the world, in which there are no differences between countries or communities. This same message is spread in the business world. Borders have disappeared, and companies increasingly benefit from the exchange of information, ideas, knowledge, or services.

The influence of technologies on business and personal activity is directly connected to their current characteristics. Increasingly, companies are concerned with knowing what their customers want and offering a credible image. Before the internet existed, users were guided by the impressions that a certain company gave them on their first contact.

Today, the relationship between company and client has changed. Users are informed in detail about the activity of each of the companies, thanks to the internet, before deciding whether to become their customers. The information that surfs the internet is available to everyone.

The main objectives of companies are; to know what customers want, what their competitors are, and how they attract the target audience, which ones they can target and with what message, how customers behave and interact with the company, and so on. The information has become an unbelievably valuable tool.

But new technologies, in addition to improving companies' internal and external communication, have also boosted their business strategies and improved their economy. Companies that use technologies for the day-to-day activities are able to save much more than those that do not. However, these same technologies can be implemented in your daily life to save quite a bit of money as well.

New technologies makes the day to day of people, and companies, easier, and helps to perform tasks faster. Likewise, new technologies also helps consumers and businesses to save. How?

One of the biggest expenses that both businesses and households face on a monthly basis are electricity and water bills. These are fixed costs that we cannot eliminate, but we can reduce thanks to the use of new technologies. An amazingly effective method is to use the lighting and heating automation system, for example, through the smartphone itself.

We can install applications that allow us to have a more exhaustive control of the consumption of light or electricity. They are known as consumer monitors and allow us to save up to 18% on the invoice or receipt.

These consumption meters or monitors, provide us with information on the energy we consume per day, providing us with reports on weekly and/or monthly consumption. Some of them can store this data on a computer in the form of a data table or graphs. In this way, we know in depth the total volume of consumption that we consume per day and opens the possibility of taking more concrete measures to reduce energy expenditure and save up to $300 a year.

As for heating, smart thermostats can be installed. These devices are capable of detecting consumption habits and the characteristics of the rooms in order to control energy consumption. They lower the temperature when they detect that the environment is already warm, so it guarantees energy efficiency and cost savings. Furthermore, you can control the temperature directly from a mobile application.

We can also make use of smart gadgets. They are able to detect when an electronic device is not being used to turn it off, such as a computer. For offices, it is a great advantage since breaks are often made. During that time, computers are not consuming energy. A gadget with this function is the Eco button, which connects to the computer via USB.

In the same way, there are smart gadgets that turn off the light when they detect that there is nobody in the room or any other device that is connected. Most devices have a motion sensor and an adapter for plugs. At a particular moment, when the said sensor does not detect any movement after the time set by the user, it sends a signal to the plug adapter so that the power is cut and, with it, the connected devices. Before doing so, it generates a beep to warn the user so that they have time to cancel the action if they wish.

New technologies has opened up the possibilities of sharing information in a much faster and more economical way. Thanks to the "cloud," members of a company or customers can transmit information in real-time without having to pick up a phone or go to a specific place. In this way, companies manage to save on the telephone bill and on trips (gasoline, train or plane tickets, etc.).

In the same way, the "cloud" allows storing large amounts of information. Businesses no longer need multiple storage devices to expand the capabilities of storing relevant data. Previously, companies spent a lot of money on buying multiple computers, hard drives, or other storage devices. With the arrival of new technologies, this expense has been reduced.

Another advantage generated by the arrival of new technologies to companies is teleworking. Thanks to electronic devices, communication between two separate points can be done in real-time, just like with business tasks. This trend has given rise to the jobs whose activity is carried out from home.

With teleworkers, companies manage to save on the electricity bill and the purchase of material or resources. You do not have to buy as many computers, chairs, and tables or rent an oversized office. In addition, telecommuting also saves energy.

Apart from that, there are several different technologies that you can integrate into your life which will help you save quite a bit of money. Some of these are as follows.

Management software: Nowadays we do not even have to spend money to have a good management software since there are a few that are free and work perfectly. These types of programs allow us to closely monitor our personal finances. We can even link them with our bank details and manage from there all our money, bills, etc.

Most often use genuinely nice interfaces with all kinds of graphics to first distinguish the state of our finances.

Smart meters: They are putting everyone's mouth on the subject of the electricity bill, but the truth is that they have been with us for a while. These types of counters are a great tool to achieve greater savings. Applied to the subject of electrical energy, we have meters that allow us to control the amount of energy we use, judge the efficiency of some electronic devices, and allow us to implement tactics to reduce our consumption.

We can also find them to control the heating system of our home. That will allow us to program it, regulate the temperature, etc.

Even today, we can find smart meters that incorporate control via Wi-Fi that will allow us to remotely control certain aspects such as light level, etc.

Instant messaging: I think we could no longer live without this type of application on our mobile phone. If you counted all the messages you sent per day through them and realized what you would spend per day if they were traditional SMS, you would shake.

Applications like WhatsApp, Skype, Telegram, etc. they save us a lot of money throughout the year. They have considerably reduced the cost of communications.

Online brokers

Online investment tools have also been a revolution. Today we can invest through these platforms from anywhere in the world and much cheaper than in the past. Commissions have been reduced incredibly in recent years.

Even today, financial advisory costs have been reduced because more and more online investment platforms appear where users themselves are helping each other.

VOIP telephony

It is surely the future of mobile tariffs. VOIP technology simply refers to services that allow us to make phone calls over an internet connection. That is, we will have to have a data connection on our mobile. The cost of this type of call is much cheaper than that of a traditional call.

Ebooks

Many people already have an iPad, Kindle, and another type of device that allows reading books in electronic format. These types of books are usually cheaper than physical ones, and therefore, if you read books frequently, it can be a good source of savings for you. In addition to this mode, you also save space on your shelf.

Technology has opened the door to the free selection of how much we want to spend. This is the revolution of revolutions that started in 2001 when iTunes decided to offer the purchase of a single song for $ 0.99. And who did not buy a complete CD to end up listening to only one song? In this sense, the internet has been presented in your favor because it has given the consumer the possibility of choosing not only what really interests him or her but also how much the individual wants to spend.

But the benefit of the selection has been reflected in all scenarios because, as for example, in the gaming industry, and it is that also you no longer have to travel to Las Vegas or Monte Carlo to play in a casino, now you can do it online. Not only that, on certain platforms, but you can also decide how much your loss limit is and configure the 'Predictive Tool' to monitor the behavior of your bets. Just like this example, there are other forms of entertainment that have also changed to help us save. For instance, do you remember when going to the cinema meant investing in a single movie? Today, thanks to the subscriptions offered by platforms like Netflix, you can watch as much as you want!

But if this were not enough, there are apps that were designed to make you save in any field. From the platform that facilitates savings for your wedding, to the one that allows you to obtain a benefit for renting your home, to some that allow you to choose what your savings goal is and achieve it through your routine purchases. In short, technology has opened an infinite universe of savings.

Chapter 8 – Your Way Out of Debt

All of us have been under debt of some type at some point in our lives. But now more than ever, debt is ubiquitous. Apart from children, people from every age group, gender and nationality share this common financial problem. It would not be wrong to say that debt is one of the biggest financial challenges in contemporary times if not the biggest.

Although debt is pervasive all around the globe, the United States has gained popularity in the context of debt. Let us have a look at some statistics from the USA.

80% of all the U.S. households have a debt of some kind. Most borrow for housing, second in line is credit card debt and thirdly, student loans.

All of the money owed by Americans sums up to $12.58 Trillion, the magnitude of this sum can be understood by the fact that it is greater than the entire GDP of China.

22% of people have more debt on their credit cards than they have savings.

Debt itself is not a bad thing at all; it allows us to own our own homes, cars and go to college. What, in fact, is bad is the situation where it brings us when we are unable to pay back. What is making matters even worse is that the vast majority of people seriously underestimate the amount of debt they're in. Because they do not check on their financial standing, they remain utterly oblivious to the fact that they owe a large amount of money in different types of loans.

Does debt cause mental problems, or do psychological problems cause debt? The best answer to this question researchers has come up with is a 'Yes' to both parts of the issue. Some research concludes that stressing about debt make you prone to mental illness. However, other studies have found that psychological problems decrease self-control, which messes up an individual's finances.

When we talk about "mental illness" related to debt, we are not referring to a full-fledged severe condition like schizophrenia. The problems one may experience are less intense; however, they can still lead you to mess up your situation further and sink deeper in debt.

Behavioral spending problems can induce you to spend without check; this will drive you into debt just as certainly as a financial emergency like sudden unemployment. The psychological issues caused by debt, and how they can lead you deeper in debt are the most significant reason why you need to get yourself out of such a situation ASAP. This chapter is all about how.

Assessing Your Situation

Before we start figuring out our way out of debt, we must try and assess our financial situation. This includes checking our monthly income and expenditure, our credit reports, credit score and most importantly, the entire amount of money we owe. After we have had a good look at our situation, we can figure out how to manage the money we already have in the best way to get out of debt quickly. Although the first chapter contains in-detail information on how to figure out your financial situation, here is a summary for you if you skipped.

Compare your monthly expenditure and income—Ready yourself for a surprise. Many people do not realize the amount of money they should be ideally spending relative to their income. By making this comparison, you can easily recognize whether you can afford your current lifestyle or not. If you find that you have a great deal of debt that you need to pay back and your contributions towards paying back are not nearly enough, you must reduce your spending. To meet your financial liabilities, you may have to do more than that, contingent on the severity of your financial state of affairs.

Review your credit reports. Your credit report is a complete catalogue of your financial situation. It contains data about how much money you owe, to whom, whether you pay it on time, whether you've exceeded your credit limits, and more. Order your credit reports from the three credit reporting agencies and take time to go through them; this will tell you all you need to know about all the money you owe.

Find out your credit score. The FICO score, which is calculated from your credit reports is a measure of your financial well-being and responsibility towards your liabilities. Moneylenders will make decisions about whether to lend you money. They will charge you interest based on this score rather than going through the entire reports. A low credit score means you will be charged higher interest on your loans and vice versa.

How to Figure Out the Entire Debt Balance?

Ordering and going through your credit reports is just an aerial view of the procedure. To find out the exact details of each of your debts and the sum of all your debts, you will need to follow these steps:

Obtain credit reports.

Enlist All the Active Accounts. The credit report shows not only the open accounts, but also those accounts that are discharged, charged off, or fully paid. When you want to calculate the total amount of money you owe, you would want to concentrate on the open accounts; these are the accounts from which creditors would try to collect. If a debt is charged off, this means that the original lender is no longer trying to collect from you. However, collecting agencies will still be pursuing the debt if the statute of limitations on the debt has not expired yet. On the contrary, if a debt is discharged, it can be no longer collected, you can leave it out. If you have a credit card account and you owe some money there, but it's not mentioned on the report, you should still go on and include that in your total debt balance.

Get in Touch with your Creditors. Call each of your creditors or log in online to all of your open accounts and find out the current balance you owe. You will also have access to other information like the interest rate and monthly payments; jot these down as this information will help you make a better debt payoff plan.

Look Out for Any Debt Not Listed on the Report. Companies sometimes do not inform the credit reporting firms about the money you owe. This not a very common problem, but just to be on the safe side, you should include any debt not included in your reports.

Add up. Once you have enlisted all balances on every account, including mortgages, credit cards, and personal loans, simply add them up, and you will know your total debt. Remember, as you pay it off, this balance will go down, but not by the entire amount of your payment; this is because a part of your payment is allocated to covering the interest.

Budgeting and Taking the Right Steps

The process of paying back your loan should ideally start as soon as you borrow the money. When you get a loan, you should spend the money wisely, so you do not face minimal difficulty paying it off in the future.

Managing the borrowed money

To make the most urgent payments first: As soon as you get the money, you should keep in mind the primary purpose of borrowing the cash. Make the payments you have to make ASAP to avoid your credit score from dropping more. If you have taken a loan to pay your rent, pay it as soon as you get the cash without getting distracted. If you have several bills at hand, take a moment and evaluate the urgency of each one. The first payments you should make are groceries, childcare, and medical bills. Second in line should be your rent. Thirdly, pay your utility bills and transport costs.

Don't spend the borrowed money unreasonably. Consider this, after you have made all your immediate payments, and you have no bills to pay until your next payday, do not let your desires destroy your resolve. When you see those brand-new heels you wanted, it becomes tough to restrain yourself when you know that you have more than enough money for yourself until payday. The key to situations like this is never to forget that you are in debt, and someone who owes even the least amount of cash should not make non-essential transactions. Whenever you find yourself in such a situation, you should remind yourself never to borrow more than you need in the first place. In the case of having extra money at hand, you should carefully save it to quickly payback by making more than the least monthly or weekly instalments.

Tips To Payback Loans

Pause for a moment to decide which kind of debt you hold – whether it's credit card debt, student debt, consumer debt or anything else – to evaluate how much obligation you have before you start paying back. Knowing the amount and type of your debts can bring you closer to a customized debt repayment plan.

Try the tips below if you are looking for quick ways to reduce your debt, including practical tweaks to your debt reduction plans and strategies.

Develop a proper plan:

You need to develop a well-thought-out plan after evaluating the details of all the money you owe. Consider the monthly payments for each of your loans, and their respective interest rates to allocate a specific sum that you would include in your budget. In the list of your monthly expenses, you should set a place for debt servicing and consider the total money you would be paying towards debt each month.

Next, pay off the largest and most expensive debt:

Now here comes the sorting part. What you need to do is start sorting the interest rates of your credit card from maximum to minimum interest rate. By first clearing off the debt with the maximum interest, this is how you can increase the credit card payment at the highest annual percentage rate while continually making the minimum payment on the majority of your credit cards.

Pay more than the least balance:

It is an appealing thing: to only pay the least amount of money each month and then having the rest for yourself. This way you can postpone the payment for a month, and then you can spend the cash as you like. But it's the wrong choice; paying the least sum not only keeps you under debt for a more extended period, but it also results in you paying more in interest and drops your credit score. Contrarily, if you pay more than the minimum amount, you will pay off the debt sooner and with a higher credit score.

Improve your ability to pay off everything by making the payments every week rather than monthly. And let's say your minimum amount is $150, now try doubling it and paying off $300 or more.

Halt your credit card spending:
Want to stop stacking up debt? Now disable all the credit card from your wallet and drop them at home while going for shopping or lunch. Even though you earn extra money or other bonuses by purchasing through a credit card, stop spending on your credit card till you have your budget and finance under control

Use work incentives and bonuses towards debt:
If you are getting a work incentive during or throughout the holidays, transfer the money to your debt repayment plan. Avoid investing the extra money on an extended vacation or other luxuries.

Remove credit card credentials from online shops:
When you do a lot of shopping online at one website, you may have saved your credit card information on the site to ease the purchase process. Sometimes it also ends up charging items you do not want to buy. So, if you opt for a recurring service, use a debit card provided from a major credit card service connected to your checking account.

Sell unnecessary goods and household items:
Do you have any Christmas presents or old wedding gifts gathering dust inside your attic? Find things you can sell online, on any trusted selling platform. Do a little research to ensure that products are offered at a fair and reasonable price.

Adjust and modify your habits:
Your daily practices and activities are the reason you get into debt. Spend a little time thinking about just how you spend your money every day, every week and every month. "Why do you need your cappuccino every day? Do you think you need it? Wouldn't it be better to bring your snacks or something for lunch to work? Rather than buying unhealthy meals 3-6 times a week? Question yourself. What can I alter without losing too much on my lifestyle?

Award yourself for achieving goals and milestones:
So, if you assume your debt as a form of torture and punishment, you will not be able to pay off your debt fast. Instead, make paying off your debt a goal and praise yourself as you hit the targets of debt payouts. "The only way of paying off your credit card debt entirely is to retain it, but to do that; you must be empowered and motivated."

When to Consider Bankruptcy?

When taking out a loan, everybody has all the intentions to pay it back on time. But things do not always go as planned. If you had taken out loans and now you see yourself drowning in debt and do not see any light at the end of the tunnel, you are not alone. Anything can happen, there's a long list of unfortunate situations that may arise; you may lose your job, you may get demoted, your financial partner may pass away – we don't want to scare you, but these are all the reasons that can strangle you and drown you in debt.

You are certainly looking for solutions to get yourself out of this precarious situation. But you need to look at all your options, bankruptcy being one of them. On the surface, it may seem like it is not an option for you; however, as you scratch the surface, you may discover that it's your best option. Here is how to figure out if you need to file bankruptcy:

When your Payments Don't Make a Difference: If you are making your debt repayments, but still the debt balance shows no signs of declining, you might want to consider bankruptcy. In the worse cases, the debt balance may even rise due to the interest even as you make your scheduled payments. In situations like these, filing bankruptcy is more important. Similarly, consider getting legal advice if you find yourself unable to make the minimum payments on your accounts. If your monthly budget is leaving you short of making all of your minimum payments, consult a credit counselling agency about getting a reduction in your payment plan. If monthly payments are still out of reach, consider filing bankruptcy.

When you are Damaging your Retirement Plans to Pay Debt: The nearer you are to your retirement age, the riskier it is to take from your retirement savings. If you are using up your retirement savings to pay off your debts, do not continue doing so! Consult a bankruptcy advisor straight away. When you take money from your retirement savings, you are stealing money from the 70-year-old you and giving it to yourself now; think about it, who deserves this money more? There can be substantial penalties to taking from your retirement funds rather than learning a lesson from bankruptcy and using that lesson to make better decisions in the future. Experts warn that simply borrowing from your retirement savings to pay off your debt can cost the retired you far more than the money you could've saved by paying off the loan on time.

When Others Face a Tough Time if you don't File: Don't make your dependents suffer. When you have dependents, whether it is your children, your spouse, or parents, your financial resources drain very fast when you have dependents to take care of alongside yourself. The emergency fund and health insurance for your dependents hold greater importance rather than paying off your unsecured loans. If you see yourself sabotaging the emergency fund plan or not paying for insurance to pay off your debts, immediately consult an advisor.

Bankruptcy is not the answer when your motive is anything other than a reasonable respite from debt. The U.S. Bankruptcy Code was established to support the honest debtors, not to support scammers and cheaters. If someone wants to bother a creditor, sneak out of debt, dodge child support, or generally just steal from someone, bankruptcy is not for people like this. No one should employ bankruptcy for taking revenge, as a temporary hack, or as a negotiating chip. You should not file for bankruptcy unless you are in a serious situation.

What can you Gain?

Stops Creditors from Taking Action Against You: As soon as you file a bankruptcy petition, a protective shield called an automatic stay starts protecting you from all sorts of troubles creditors may cause for you. It inhibits creditors from contacting you regarding your loans, filing a case against you, taking over your property and your wages.

With an automatic stay in place, the creditor would need permission for the repossession of property or for foreclosure. The judge will likely disallow the creditor to take any actions if you come up with a logical plan to pay the debt. Furthermore, if any creditor makes a mistake to ignore your automatic stay, they will be fined and ordered to pay your attorney fees too.

Wipes Out Debts: Filing bankruptcy will wipe out or discharge most of your debts. Medical bills, credit cards, phone expenses, loans, and judgments all are typically removed. However, there are some types of loans that are not dischargeable, such as student loans, child support, taxes and fines.

Catch Up on Vehicle Loans and Back Mortgage: If you file a Chapter 13 bankruptcy, you can come up with a partial-repayment strategy to prevent foreclosure and make up the back-mortgage payments in five years. You can also stop seizure of your vehicle this way. In some cases, you will pay only what the car is worth rather than the whole loan.

Chapter 13 Bankruptcy to Pay Debts Over Time. Some debts cannot be discharged; however, by filing a Chapter 13 bankruptcy, you can pay debts like support obligations or back taxes over five years. It also keeps you from being pressurized while you are paying off the money. This enables you to catch up on the missed mortgage payments progressively. At the same time, most of the other debts are discharged, and you will just pay for present expenditures and keep current on the future house and vehicle payments.

Repay All Your Debt: Sometimes, bankruptcy provides a way for you to pay all of your debts rather than evading them. If the worth of your property is enough to pay all the money you owe only if you had time enough to sell it, you could utilize bankruptcy to keep creditors at bay so you can sell your property. On top of that, you can even keep the surplus for yourself.

For instance, you own investment assets worth $100,000, you have a mortgage of $50,000, and other debts are summing up to $25,000. If you could sell these assets, you can not only pay off the mortgage and other obligations, but you will also have something left over for yourself. Contrarily, if the mortgage holder forecloses, you will not be able to get a cent nor any of your lenders. Filing bankruptcy will interrupt the foreclosure process so you can sell the property for everyone's benefit.

What can you Lose?

You Can Lose Property: There is a possibility that you can lose your property by filing bankruptcy; however, it is highly unlikely and depends on the worth of the particular property and its location.

Bankruptcy is Public: Records are stored on the internet, and it has become even easier for anyone interested to look these up. Simply put, anyone can know whether you have filed bankruptcy or not, the amount of money you owe, and to whom.

Bankruptcy Damages your Credit Score: Filing bankruptcy will have an adverse impact on your credit reports and will lead to a lower credit score. But when you actually are filing bankruptcy due to logical reason, your credit score and the impact of bankruptcy on it does not hold much importance.

You can Suffer Discrimination. Governmental authorities and employers aren't expected to discriminate against you over bankruptcy; however, they may still do so, one way or the other. Employers might also decide against hiring you if they see you have filed bankruptcy.

Chapter 9 – Invest in Your Future

You might often wonder, should you save or should you invest? Although the answer to this is a bit complicated, we certainly do know this, that saving is also a type of investing, it's investing in your future. Both saving and investing defer consumption of money from the present to the future. When we talk about investing in your future, we refer to all those practices which you allocate money to now, and you will reap the benefits later.

Investing in your future includes savings, investments in the form of bonds and shares, investing in your or your kids' education and so on. In this chapter will thoroughly go through all the aspects of saving, investing and identify the common mistakes people make in doing so.

Some of you might be a long way from a pro-savings mindset; here are some reasons to convince you that saving and investing in your future is more important than you think.

The older-you deserves the money more than the present you. Save now so your retirement – AKA Golden Years – is secure. You use the youthful energy right now to protect a pleasant future. Each dollar you put aside today will count in the years to come. Over the years, you are guaranteed to get more money than what you invested now: a motivation for you. When the retirement age comes, it brings along its fair share of changes. A lot of things you worry about now will not be a much of a priority then. This way, you will be able to relax and utilize your money to the maximum.

Your family is secured. The best and the most challenging part of having a family is to take care of them. By investing now, you prepare a relaxed life for them when you do not have enough strength to. When you are old, you'll have the time, and the money, to do whatever you want. It is never too late to start saving. When you have a family, they also benefit from savings. You won't be forced to live with your children due to being financially unstable, and this can be really straining for them. This may be hard to realize now, but it is honest advice from people who have already been through this. Save now to secure your future and so that everyone is happy.

Saving Under Debt

To many readers, this statement might come as a complete surprise. But as unbelievable this seems to you; it is an even more practical and useful financial exercise. However, this is only possible when you can make regular monthly or weekly payments. You cannot save unless you are paying the more immediate obligations first.

When you are making the monthly payments to repay a student loan or any other kind of debt, you might be thinking that you cannot save money as long you pay off your debt. On the contrary, financial experts claim that you should still be saving money even as you pay the debt because it can be really beneficial for you.

The primary reason that supports the idea of saving while under debt is that the money you save will grow with time. The more time you give it, the more money you will have by the end of your savings plan. Financial experts and researchers claim that a vast majority of people often spends a significant proportion of their life paying off student loans and other debts they took early on in their financial careers. Paying off large loans of the sort can take decades over decades to pay back in full, and when you wait that long to start saving, you often end up with little or even nothing by retirement age.

Furthermore, saving while in debt is also essential in the short term. If you allocate all your money apart from your current expenses towards the repayment of loans, you will be left with nothing in case of an emergency. When you have nothing to yourself and pay all you have to creditors, you will find yourself in a very problematic situation.

Consider this, you had $2,000 left from your salary, and you pay the $1,800 to a creditor, and keep only $200 to yourself. Suppose a medical emergency comes up and you have got a $1000 bill on your hands, what are you going to do? Where are you going to go? You cannot ask your lender to give you the money back, neither do you have any savings, now what? You may be forced to take out another loan, increasing your debt and repeating the cycle all over again.

Here is a plan for you to save money in debt:

Pay attention to the Interest Rates: The most critical factor when it comes to evaluating your financial priorities is the rate of interest on the money you owe. The highest interest rates belong to credit card debts, with a national average of 12.8%. Student loans come second with interest rates lower than 10%. We must consider these high-interest debts before we start to save because all the money you save now will go to waste in order to pay the cost of the high interest. So, before you begin saving, eliminate the high-interest loan first. On the other hand, if you are paying a loan with a lesser interest rate such as student loan, you can utilize the extra money by saving it.

Refinance your Student Debt: Lower interest rates will help you save more. One excellent option to drop the interest rate even lower on your student loan is to refinance it. Refinancing means replacing your existing debt with another loan under different terms. You can refinance your student loan and get a new loan through a private creditor, this way you can get interest rates as low as 2%. However, for doing so, you need an excellent credit score. You should bear in mind that, by refinancing, you give up your federal loan protections which include loan forgiveness, income-based repayment plans, forbearance, and deferment. If you decide to take this route, whenever you notice a rise in your FICO score, you can refinance your loans again, this time to an even lower interest rate. Furthermore, refinancing typically involves a refinancing charge. To evaluate whether refinancing your loan is worth its cost, examine your outstanding balance. If you have a substantial amount of money still left to be paid, such as $80,000, a lower interest will help you a lot. However, if little remains to be paid, you should not waste your money on refinancing. One benefit of refinancing again from the same private lender as the first time, you will not have to pay the transaction fee back. Contingent on your outstanding balance, refinancing could save you a lot of money that would've otherwise be spent on paying interest you can use this money for saving and investing.

Take a Personal Loan: If you have a lot of credit card debt on high-interest rates, taking a personal loan on much cheaper terms is the way to go. When you get money at a much lower interest rate than what you're receiving on the credit card debt, you can utilize the funds from the personal loan to pay off the credit card debt right away and then pay off the new loan at the much lower interest rate relatively easily. One thing you need to bear in mind is that you require a good credit score to qualify for the low-interest personal loan.

Use Automation: You should automate your debt repayments for a variety of reasons. First of all, it saves you money which you would otherwise lose to paying late fees or other unnecessary charges. Furthermore, by using a debt auto repayment strategy, federal loan services may give you a 0.25% reduction in your interest rate. But what seems to be the most important benefit of debt repayment automation is that it takes your mind off the money you owe and puts it onto the money you need to save. At the beginning of this eBook, we discussed the role of the Law of Attraction in your financial situation. You should know that by constantly thinking and wondering about your debt and paying it off will attract more of it into your life; automation will ensure this no longer happens.

Investing

We invest where the value will grow with time, and we will get the benefits for our financial matters. We always take some risk while investing. If our investment over time is positive, it can be gratifying. We will discuss investment risks later in this chapter. Here, we must know that there are some basics and categories in investment, for example, cash investment, investments in bonds and the stock market. In each of these categories, you invest your money using various approaches.

Cash equivalent investments include a certificate of deposits (CDs) and US treasury bills. You can invest in mutual funds and exchange-traded funds. If the investment money isn't readily available to cover financial emergencies, you will be concerned about liquidity, or how quickly it can be turned to cash with minor or no less of value or deductions. But when investing for longer-term goals, liquidity holds much less importance. The most liquid investments are CDs, treasury bills, and saving accounts which generally provide the lowest return/profit. Still, in case your money is secure, and they offer more safety. In this case, the risk is much less.

Identify How Much Money You Can Invest?

If you do not know how much money you can manage to invest, then your investment plan is lacking. Try to preserve your savings and even open another saving account making it your account that you use for investment savings; and don't spend all of them. You need to work according to your financial goals. See if your income is going to give you some additional money to invest or not. Try to consult a professional broker; he will guide you about the branches of investments and how much you can get benefit from it. Depending upon the types of investments, you can make a yearly plan according to the money you have for investment. When you are going to choose a broker, check his license to avoid any kind of difficulties. Brokers earn from the commissions on sales, and they decide their set percentage of the transaction. The two types of brokers are full-service brokers and discount brokers. The full-service brokers give you pieces of advice and make offers of various investments. Whereas the ones who do not provide any kind of advice and don't study regarding it are the discount brokers. Invest money where it is safe to invest, do not waste your money on risky investments and ventures.

When you have decided to invest, you must do your homework; that is research about the investment opportunity. You must research it and observe how earlier investors have done as well. There are countless books and websites on the topic, and you can even take college-level courses on the subject. Many influential decision-makers are connected to financial markets; you can contact them and take their opinions.

Investing in Stocks

When you buy a share of the stock of a company, you have partial ownership of it. That is, a part of its properties and its revenue. One share does not signify a large enough piece of ownership for the average public company, which might have millions of shares outstanding. For instance, General Motors has more than 566 million shares issued on the market. The more shares you have in a company, the larger the part of the company you own. Someone who owns stock is called a shareholder.

A stock has no absolute value. They are equity investments that represent part ownership in a corporation and entitle you to be a part of that corporation earning's and assets. Its value depends upon shareholder's decision whether they want to sell it or hold it. You must know about the availability of stocks before going into the market. Diversification is provided to you while investing in the stock market. Check out the company's financial statements on the SSC's website before investing. Due to the lack of reliable info about the company's financial matters. It is up to you to make decisions about investments to match your desired goals.

Stock marketing seems to be complicated. It is not that difficult how people think about it. Stock market investing includes these two types, i.e. stock mutual funds (exchange-traded funds) or individual stocks.

Stock mutual funds are also called equity mutual funds. You can buy small parts of multiple different stocks in exchange-traded funds. These can be finished in a single transaction. Whereas in individual stocks, you can buy a single share. It takes a notable investment to construct a diversified portfolio out of multiple individual stocks.

After that, you need to set up a budget for stock market investment. The earlier you will determine what amount of money you have to invest in the stock market, the more beneficial it will be for you because the prices of the stocks depend upon the shares. You can also take advice about how much money you can invest at that time from your financial planner. He will guide you about the ups and downs of the stock market.

It is difficult to invest with a small amount of money. The less money you will have, the harder it will be for you to invest. So, make sure to have a sufficient amount of money before investing. It does not mean you cannot invest if you don't have enough money, you can invest in stock index funds. It is an excellent opportunity for beginners to start their investment plans through stock market investment.

There are two broad categories of earning money through stocks. One is when the overall price of a share increases, and you sell it off to make a profit. The second way is through dividends; you get part of the profit the company earns without selling your shares. The difference between the two is that earning by dividends is usually a prolonged process as companies only offer a very tiny proportion of the profit of the company to the shareholders, while you can sell stock as soon as the price rises and you'll earn. When you are investing, you will keep ownership of the shares for a long time, hence, not only will you receive the dividend over time, you can sell the shares later on at a much higher price, given that the firm you've invested in grows.

Investing in Bonds

Bonds are loans that investors give to corporations and governments. Bonds sometimes work better than bank loans. In this investment, people get low-interest rates, but the risk is lowest. The numerous types of bond funds include mutual funds, closed-end funds, exchange-traded funds, and unit investment trust. Bond funds allow investors to purchase an executively selection and managed a portfolio of bonds with a single investment.

A bond is a debt security. Borrowers issues bonds to raise money from investors willing to lend them cash for a certain amount of time. You are supplying to the issuer by purchasing a bond. A government, municipality, or corporation can be a bond issuer. An issuer promises the specified rate of interest during the life of the bond and to repay the principle also known as face value or par value of the bond, after the maturity or comes due after a set period.

This provides a facility for preserving assets and earning a predictable return. This investment offers steady streams of income from interest payments before maturity. The interest or profits from municipal bonds are generally exempted from federal income tax and also may be exempted from government and local taxes for residents where the bond is issued. As with any investment bonds, there are risks. These risks include credit risks, interest rate risks, inflation risk, liquidity risk, and call risk.

In the credit risk, the issuer may fail to pay interest or principal payments and thus defaults on its bonds. The bonds are also affected by interest rate changes.

The general upward movement in prices is inflation. It reduces the purchasing power of buyers. This is also a risk for investors receiving a fixed rate of the amount.

Liquidity risk refers to the risk that investors won't find a market for the bond, potentially preventing them from buying and selling when they need or want to.

Call risk is the possibility that a bond issuer retires a bond before its maturity date, something an issuer might do if interest rate declines. For instance, a land or homeowner might refinance an already mortgaged to benefit from lower interest rates.

Common Mistakes People Make While Investing

When people are new to the investing business, they have little knowledge and only know the very basics of investing. For instance, you might be thinking about buying some shares, and you might have the perception that stock marketing is merely a matter of luck. You buy now, the price of the shares rises, and you will be rich pass one year. Things don't always go in your favour, and that being a fact, you will be able to gain more from your investment if you keep yourself actively engaged with your shares and not by staying aloof and expecting to be wealthy after some time. By spending time in setting your investment goals and customizing your investment plan, you can minimize the risks and maximize the profits.

You can lose money when you invest – you need to accept this. Here are the five primary reasons why people lose money in their investments, so you know never to make these mistakes.

Investing Without Preparation: Having a few extra hundred bucks in your wallet does not mean you are ready to invest your money. Your priority should be a healthy savings and emergency fund so you can deal with any financial problems while simultaneously having invested your money in the stock market or bonds. There are two primary reasons for this:

When you find yourself in a financial emergency, you need money fast, and when you do not have the money in the emergency fund, you'll be forced to sell your stock. Although shares are relatively liquid assets, you might be forced to sell your stock at a loss because you need the money immediately.

If you have any outstanding balance, you should pay those obligations first. This is because the profit you may earn from your investment would be less than the cost of interest you will incur by not paying off the debts. So, you go in a loss.

Investing Without Direction: Before you invest, you need to set your goals. You need to know where you want to go and what you want to achieve from your investment. If you do not, how are you going to differentiate if you've achieved what you wanted or not?

Not Doing Your Homework: Believing in 'hot tips' has led many investors to lose a lot of money. When you hear a rumour that the stock of a company is going to skyrocket very soon and if you buy without giving it a good thought and research, you will lose money, a lot of it.

Putting All Your Eggs in One Basket: Consider this, you invest all the money you have in the stock of one particular company, and it goes well for the first few years. There you think that you have got your retirement all covered, but suddenly something happens, and that company declares bankruptcy and the price of the stock plummets. You break all your eggs. Do not do this. Diversify your portfolio. Invest in the stocks of various companies, in bonds and mutual funds to keep yourself safe.

Following the Herd: If everyone is selling their stock, do not sell yours too. If everyone is buying a stock, do not put your money in the same place. Always act on your own accord, take your own steps that you have backed with logic and research. Winners always stand out. And even if you lose, you will regret more when you lose following someone else rather than yourself.

Investing in Education

Are you expecting reading about investing in the education sector? Well, that is a very sound opportunity and is bound to earn you profits. But this sub-chapter is not about investing in other people's education; it is about investing in your own and your family's education.

No amount of money, resources, contacts or power can give you what a good education can. In fact, all of the four things are dependent on education; and unfortunately, not many people today realize the value of education. Spending money in your education or your children's' education seems like the most long-term investment there is, and it seems like it may not pay off every time. But believe this, if and when it does, every penny you spend towards education is going to come back, many times multiplied.

Enough of the lecture, let's discuss the technicalities. College and paying for it is what seems to be the most significant part of investing in education. Many American households keep a college fund, and many American kids still do not get to go to college. Primary and secondary school is free but undergraduate and postgraduate is not, and the latter is what matters the most today. Save for college now, and do not make yourself or your kids take a student loan and spend their whole lives paying it off.

To efficiently save for college, you need to figure out the approximate cost of your dream college and how much time do you have left. If you are a parent, show responsibility and start as soon as you can. Apart from savings, scholarships are a perfect opportunity to attend college. If you or your children manage to secure good scholarships, attending college would be effortless.

Chapter 10 – Protecting What You Have

Working hard to earn a living, sacrificing your wishes for a better tomorrow, all those budgets and savings plans, what if all that went to waste? In the olden days, people physically hurt other people when they wanted to harm them. Today when somebody wants to harm you, they simply take your financial life away. Today, the world is full of financial dangers and setback risks. It is entirely up to you whether you want to keep your hard-earned money safe from financial predators or leave the door open for the wolf.

Identity Theft

We often take our freedom for granted. We think that tomorrow is going to be much like today. But it does not matter when you have been a target of identity theft. While you are entirely unaware, someone can steal your private information and can commit any scam using your name. Identity theft is so severe that you could be charged with any scam which you do not even know about, it can harm your reputation in the society. The victims of identity theft are forced to pay money and carried by different false charges. Having your identity stolen will cost you money in so many ways. As we have already discussed, identity theft can lead you to an even bigger problem: the damage it does to your credit score.

Maintaining a good credit score is a very tough job. But having it fall to horrible numbers is a piece of cake. Identity theft can destroy your credit ratings in seconds, and you might take up years to recover it; all due to something you did not do.

Reduce the Risk: Finding out you are a victim of identity theft can be frightening, and a source of anxiety even after you have resolved the issue. How can you reduce the risk? What will you do if it happens to you or your family? Figuring out how scammers access your information is the first step in reducing the risk. If you have lost your wallet somewhere or it was stolen then, it is a great risk of becoming a victim of identity theft. Carrying essential documents like your identity card, credit cards, debit cards, birth certificate, driver's license in your wallet can give a thief easy access to your personal information. You shouldn't carry your birth certificate and social security card wherever you go. Always shred sensitive documents before throwing them in the garbage. If somebody steals it from there, then it will become a problem for you and the risk of identity theft will be increased.

Agents or companies that have authorized access to your personal information may use that information for non-business activities. They can misuse your private data; this is mostly outside of your knowledge and control. As always, screen your credit reports for unanticipated activity.

Spyware and Adware: Computer viruses that spy on you while you shop, doing banking or business online are extra horrible. Any website or application on which you enter personal data is going to put you near danger. There are tools available on your computer or laptop to scan this type of threat. Online purchasing at a site that is not secured can probably put you at risk of having your information stolen. Web sites may also collect and sell some of your information without your knowledge unless their official privacy policy states otherwise. Shop online at merchant sites you know and trust. Make sure they have a posted Privacy Policy that makes sense to you.

What to Do if Your Identity Is Stolen? When you find out that you have been a victim of identity theft, you must take proper and quick action. You must report identity theft immediately to one of the three major credit bureaus. You are only required to call one bureau to place the fraud alert, and they will forward the information to the other two. Reporting your account will alert creditors to protect you.

Dangers of Online Banking

Having access to your bank account on your mobile phone or PC is banking convenience at its peak. However, with its increased usage, online banking is becoming an attractive target for hackers and cyber-attacks. Over the past few years, many leading banks have been targeted by hackers. But this comes into the category of bank hacking, where thieves target the bank to steal money and not you individually.

When you bank online, you use a device, an internet connection and your secret data to log in and carry out transactions. Any person can exploit loopholes in your device and internet security system to get access to the private information such as bank account number, credit card number, your passwords and more. They can use this information to steal money from you. Here are three major risks other than identity theft of online banking and how you can protect yourself:

Phishing: You may fall victim to phishing if you have an online banking account. This approach generally involves cheating you into clicking on a link in an email. The link typically downloads malware to your computer that gathers sensitive data such as bank account numbers and passwords. Otherwise, the link may redirect you to a fake website that looks like precisely the original website. Once there, the site asks for private data that can be misused by hackers to access your accounts, such as email or social media.

Keylogging: If you access your bank account online on a public network, like an internet café or public Wi-Fi, there is a risk of falling victim to keylogging. In keylogging, a software records your keystrokes and uses this data to expose your account details to the keylogger. Keylogging can also be done by using a video camera that records the buttons you press on the keyboard.

Pharming: Although it is the most challenging way for hackers to access your information, it still poses a danger. In pharming, hackers can take over your bank's URL and replicate the original website on that URL. When you enter your details on this bogus site, you compromise all the data.

Here's what you can do keep your data safe.

Confirm that you are on the real site. Be sure that you do not fall victim to websites that use a title that is very similar to your bank. For instance, Citigrop.com or Bank of America.com. Whenever you get an email claiming to be from your bank, do not click on any links in the email right away. Alternatively, search for your bank on Google and login from there, and see whether the email was real or not. If your bank actually wants to contact you, you will find a pop-up message when you open your account. You can also directly call your bank to check if there is anything, whatever you do, do not click on that link.

You should know your bank's security system, and how your bank encrypts your private data. When you are logging in to the bank website, look for a small key or lock symbol, these icons tell you that the site and your activity is secure. Do not save your PIN or passwords in any online password manager; you should use the PIN or password every time you log in. Do not send any personal data over email or any messaging app! You should remember that your bank will never ask you for your confidential data over email or text message.

Last but not least, keep your devices protected. Banks and their websites are not always the target of cyberattacks. Many of these attacks are focused on the clients, that is you. Having the latest malware and virus scanning software on your computer will ensure that you are well protected. Make sure that all the antivirus software along with all other apps that you use on your computer are updated.

Additionally, do not get lethargic in matters of online banking. Some banking websites offer the option to 'Remember your device,' so you can log in using this device directly without any checks. By choosing this option, the bank can instantly recognize your IP address, and you will not have to input your password or other details. The problem with this is that hackers can replicate your IP address, your bank will know the hacker's computer as yours, and off goes your money and your credit score.

Home Insurance

When we talk about managing the money you already have, an essential factor that needs our attention is how we can use our money to protect our assets in other forms like property, vehicles, and other liquid or non-liquid assets. Homeowners insurance is a type of property insurance that covers losses and reparations to the place of your residence, along with the furnishings and the other property in your house. Additionally, homeowner's insurance provides liability coverage for any accidents in the house or on your property.

Your home insurance deal is one of the best and most beneficial deals you are going to make; you will be able to cover huge undesired expenses in just a matter of a few dollars. On the other hand, this deal can also prove to be one of the riskiest deals because of the high number of limitations and exclusions that are part of the agreement; with the proper knowledge and guidance, you'll be able to spend your money on the right deal for you.

When you buy an insurance deal, it is vital for you to identify the limitations of the agreement. You need to identify all that falls outside of the deal, meaning all the things that are not covered by insurance. When you know this, you can develop a plan to reduce the risk or retain the losses if and when an occurrence is not covered by insurance. Most people find out that their home is insufficiently insured only when they incur a loss and discover that insurance will not cover this. In this piece, you will read about how you can utilize home insurance to the full extent and minimize your losses. Here are the five biggest mistakes people make while insuring their home and how you can avoid them to save money.

Considering Only the Cost: One of the biggest mistakes people make in home insurance is when they consider only the cost of the deal and not its value. They are mostly concerned about the price of the premium they are going to pay instead of the coverage amount they are purchasing. When you are buying a home insurance deal, never base your decision only on the low price of premiums. Ascertain that low-cost policies are not cheaper because essential coverage is removed from them or that the insurance firm has insufficient reinsurance.

Under-Insurance: Many people buy an insurance plan only enough to cover the expense of their mortgage. However, a mortgage is usually 80-90% of the value of the property at most, and it is even lesser if the price of the property has risen. Some homeowners insure an amount only equal to the current price of their property. But the present value of may be much less than the price of rebuilding it. This is especially true in the case of a natural disaster when the cost of labor and building materials hits the sky. You are recommended to calculate the cost of rebuilding your home and insure to that sum.

Not Having Flood Insurance: Many people automatically assume that they are covered by their insurance in case of a flood, while in reality, they are not. Flood coverage is not included in a standard homeowners' insurance plan. Even if it is not necessary to buy flood insurance in your area, you still are at risk of flooding. Do not think you are entirely safe from floods; hurricanes Irene and Sandy caused inland flooding as inland as New England, even in Vermont. On top of that, when you live in a low-risk area, the cost of insurance is also low. You require a 30-day wait after purchasing the deal, so homeowners do not wait it out for bad weather.

Undervaluing your Property: You are recommended to carry out an inventory of personal possessions and valuable items. Most policies seriously limit the amount of money you will receive to replace your belongings and restrict or even exclude everyday household things from your insurance deal. If you have an agreement that pays the cash value on your possessions, you will get a check for what your property was worth, not the cost to replace them.

Expecting Coverage on Things that are not: Many home insurance policies do not cover mold damage or remediation, or sewage problems, those who do are limited. Sewage backup insurance is typically a low-cost supplementary. Figure out if your property is at risk depending on its age, place and humidity levels.

Car Insurance

Car insurance is an integral part of car ownership. A car is the most dangerous machine you own unless you keep a gun with you everywhere you go. Quicker than you can imagine, you can have law cases, fatality, disability, substantial health expenses, and property damage. Therefore having a good car insurance plan is so important: A good insurance plan keeps you from incurring hefty financial losses following a severe accident. In this piece, we will discuss how you can save money while still having a good auto insurance program.

If you have more than one car or drivers, insure them together. If you insure a single vehicle or driver individually, you will end up paying a higher price then what you would pay if you insured collectively. This simply represents the idea of bulk buying; when you buy more of a product and service, the providers offer you a lower price. This effect is magnified in the case of auto insurance as you can save a healthy sum by insuring multiple vehicles or drivers together. Car insurance companies will offer lower prices as you are bringing them more business by insuring more than one vehicle or driver.

Keep an eye out for cheaper premiums. If you must renew your annual plan and the premium has gone up significantly, you should shop around looking for more affordable premiums from competitor insurance firms. Additionally, you should check up on other premiums offered by different companies; to make certain that you do not go on paying a higher price while cheaper alternatives are available.

You should remember, cheap doesn't necessarily mean as good and opting the lower price isn't the wisest decision always. To check a particular car insurance company, you should check out a website that compares the financial strength of different insurers. Testing for the financial strength of your insurance firm is essential but knowing what your plan covers is also necessary.

Low-cost and environment-friendly cars are cheaper to insure. Buying a big SUV may be exciting but buying an insurance plan for a top-of-the-line vehicle like this can be a lot more costly than insuring a smaller low-cost car. Some insurers will also offer you a discount for insuring an eco-friendly hybrid or electric vehicle. You will feel good about caring for the atmosphere and saving money at the same time.

Raise your Deductibles. When choosing a car insurance plan, you typically have to select a deductible. A deductible is an amount of money you will have to pay before the insurance company picks up the tab for an accident, theft, or other damage to the car. On the basis of your policy, deductibles generally range from $250-1,000. The trick over here is, the lower the deductible, the higher the premium.

Contrarily, the greater the deductible, the cheaper the premium. You can ask your insurance advisor about how the premium might be affected if you increased the deductible. It might lower the price of your annual premium significantly and help you save a good amount of money, or the savings might even be nominal. If you reluctantly report smaller claims to prevent raising the premium, raising your deductible may be a brilliant move.

Your Credit Score affects your insurance plan!! It may be surprising for you to hear, but it is true. Your driving record is a significant influencer in shaping insurance costs. It obviously makes sense that someone who has had a lot of car accidents would cost the company a lot more money. But why credit ratings? Experts claim that insurance companies use this information to determine how responsible you are in general; the more responsible you are, the less likely you are to file frequent claims. Regardless of if you believe this or not, you still need to maintain a good credit score. Why not be on the safe side and markedly reduce your premium by improving your credit rating?

Life Insurance

'Love' is the 'Why' of life insurance. We love our spouse and kids and our family who are financially dependent on us. And this love makes us ponder about the harsh reality of death and what their future will be when we're no longer here to provide for them. This love is sufficient to invest our hard-earned money into insurance that will ensure that if and when we die, our passing will not lead our loved ones into hard times. Life insurance will see off that the rents are paid, there's food on the table, and that your children can go to college.

Firstly, you need to figure out whether you need life insurance in the first place. Just like someone who does not own a car doesn't need vehicle insurance. Similarly, you don't need life insurance if you don't have any dependents. If you do have dependents, and you must buy life insurance, you need to figure out how much you need.

Here is how to save money on life insurance.

Choose term insurance rather than permanent. You may think all life insurance plans act in the same way. However, there is actually a massive difference from one coverage type to the next. Lifetime plans build cash value and provide coverage for as long as you pay premiums. On the contrary, term life provides coverage for a particular number of years. After the set time has elapsed, you will renew the plan if you want to maintain the coverage. The main difference is that term life plans usually are cheaper than whole life plans. So, if you want to pay less for reliable coverage, choose life term policy.

Pay your Premiums Annually. It is not easy at all for everyone to come up with a big bunch of cash instantly. But if you can manage to pay all the money all at once, it can be your best shot at saving money while paying for your life insurance plan. Insurance companies typically add on service charges or tack the premium slightly higher if you choose to pay on a monthly or quarterly basis. So, if you want to avoid these extra expenses, opt for a single annual payment. If you think it is hard for you, just use the budgeting skills you learned in the earlier chapters. Use an envelope to deposit the monthly payments as you would if you chose a monthly payment cycle and deposit the contents of the envelope at the end of the year. You might be surprised if you save some bucks from that when you make the payment.

If You Are Healthy, Don't Buy a Guaranteed Issue. Guaranteed issue life insurance plans need no medical examination but may need to ask you a few fundamental medical questions. These insurance policies carry a higher risk for the insurance company. They are, thus, costlier than thoroughly underwritten insurance plans.

Guaranteed policies are typically bought by people who face a hard time getting life insurance due to the medical problems they have. If you have any medical issues, you are likely to get a better and cheaper life insurance rate by choosing an underwritten policy, which needs you to undergo a medical exam.

The high-priced premiums, plus a low death benefit, make the guaranteed issue life insurance plan a less preferable option. Some of these policies can make you pay more in the form of premiums only after a few years than the death benefits your beneficiaries are ever going to receive.

Chapter 11 – Dealing with Taxes

As a citizen of your country, you owe an annual sum of money to your nation. It is called tax. While many of us are reluctant to file taxes, every government ensures due payment of taxes by law. If you do not pay, you violate the law and are subject to legal action. Taxes go to the government, and they are used to pay the salaries of government employees, to pay for governmental works and other national or state expenses.

In this chapter, you will learn how to file your federal and state taxes the easy way, know your rights and how you can deal with any problems with tax collectors.

Filing Federal Taxes

Tax Day in 2020 is 15th July. If you see this date coming your way and you do not have the money in your pocket to pay your taxes, the last thing you need to do is panic. Do not just bury your head in the ground hoping for the storm to pass without hurting you. Simply ignoring your taxes when you cannot pay them will cost you a great deal.

The least you can do is file your tax return at the right time. You can look up for the IRS form 4868, which is the application for an automatic extension to file. This will give you some extra time to file your tax returns, typically 6-7 months. This does not mean you have more time to pay your taxes; taxes are supposed to be paid on the due date. If there's a delay, the collecting agency will start charging interest and penalties on the taxes you haven't settled on the very next day of Tax Day. For this very reason, you should pay all that you can on the Tax Day instead of paying nothing. The higher amount you leave unsettled on the Tax Day, the higher interest will you be charged afterwards, and you will pay more consequently.

It is a great feeling being able to pay all your taxes come Tax Day and being free of all taxes for the next year. However, if you do not have the money in your pocket to pay your federal taxes, you can use the strategies discussed below. Bear in mind that all of these are expensive ways of paying your taxes on time, and if you have other more viable options, choose them rather than the ones discussed here.

Using Your Credit Card: You will have to pay a charge of approximately 2.5% on the amount that you have charged to the tax collector. If you do not pay all of your tax loans when you get your account statement, you will have to pay interest in the form of outstanding credit. Do not just assume that you will be able to pay all your taxes with the credit card, declare bankruptcy afterwards, and make your credit card debt go away. If you have filed for bankruptcy before you pay the credit card debt due to tax, the court dealing with your bankruptcy case will see the credit card debt precisely the same way it would see your taxes if they were still unpaid. To put shortly, if the taxes can be discharged by filing bankruptcy, you can use bankruptcy to get rid of the credit card debt. On the other hand, if the taxes are not dischargeable in bankruptcy, you will not be able to use bankruptcy to get rid of the debt.

Pay Using a Credit Card Convenience Check: This choice is more expensive than the others because you will probably have to pay extra charges to your bank or credit card issuer for the facility of using a convenience check. Additionally, if you do not pay off the sum on the check at once, interest starts to accumulate.

You Can Borrow From Your Home Equity: The good thing about using this route is that the interest you are going to pay on this borrowed cash is probably tax-deductible. The bad news, however, is that if you do not pay the money you have lent, you can lose your house.

Filing State Taxes

Most of the states depend on some type of income tax to finance their expenditures. In most cases, these tax returns are rationally easy to make because they are supported by your federal returns, using either the gross income you have calculated yourself or the federal taxable income. From both of these, you can add income items that are not federally taxable, minus others, and do some simple math to figure out your state taxable income.

Some states like Colorado, Indiana, Illinois, Massachusetts, Pennsylvania, Michigan, and Utah use a flat income tax rate, while others use a graduated scale. State income tax rates are generally lower than federal tax rates; however, many states start taxing sums that are lesser than the national tax thresholds, or simply do not allow much space for deductions.

You may find out that you have pending state income tax even if you do not owe a penny to the IRS. This is because every state does not follow federal tax calculation in state income taxation. For instance, Tennessee and New Hampshire tax only interest and dividends, and not rents, wages, or capital profits. There are other states too that have no tax on personal income such as Texas, Florida, Nevada, Alaska, Wyoming, South Dakota, and Washington.

What makes preparing the state income tax returns trickier is that some sources of income that are taxed federally are not taxable on the state returns. These items mainly include the interest earned from U.S. Treasury liabilities such as U.S. Treasury notes, bonds, and bills.

Other things are not taxed on your federal returns but are taxable on the state returns, such as tax-exempt interest earned on municipal bonds from other states. So, if you are a resident of Washington and have a New York municipal bond, you will not have to pay income tax on the earned interest to the IRS, but you will have to pay tax to Washington. Furthermore, you need to remember that municipal bonds from the U.S. Virgin Islands, Puerto Rico, American Samoa, and any other U.S. territory or possession are not taxable federally and not in any state too.

If you are a resident of one state for one full year and you only own property or have shares in a business situated in that particular state, you will have to file an income tax return in that state only. Conversely, if you own a property that is rented in another state, have shares in businesses that operate in another state, or live in one state and work in another, you will have non-resident source income. You must file your taxes in a second state also. In the same way, if you shifted your residence halfway through the year from one state to another, you would have to file state returns in both the states where you lived and earned.

Do not worry about ending up paying more taxes than you were required to. All states give credit for taxes paid to the other states, so you will only pay in each state only on the income while you were living in that state or your income derived from sources inside that particular state. If you are needed to file more than one state returns, you should consult a tax advisor. They will help you calculate which state is owed what tax which can sometimes get very confusing.

Avoiding Errors

People all over the world lose millions of dollars over simple tax mistakes every year. Only if they knew the simple laws, they would never have lost their money in wasteful interest charges and fines. You do not have to read tax laws and understand all that tax jargon to know these laws. We have summarized them for you in simple prose so you only have to give one read and you're set to go! Here are the ten most common tax mistakes and how to avoid them.

Not Filing On Time: Tax collecting agencies like the IRS in the USA estimate that 20% taxpayers delay filing their tax returns until only a week before the annual tax deadline. Regrettably, waiting until the eleventh hour can lead some procrastinators to miss the tax deadline if they experience any unforeseen circumstances or problems in the week before Tax Day.

You can apply for a filing extension, and this will give you more time to file the returns. However, you still need to pay all the taxes on the original tax date, which is 15th of April 2020 for the tax year 2019. In the case of failure in making the payments in due time, you will be charged interest and other fines.

Not Providing the Correct Information, or Not Providing at All: One of the most frequent tax filing errors is leaving an information box blank or entering incorrect data. One particular mistake is when you miss or mistake a digit in your social security number. Mistakes like these can delay the processing of your tax returns and can make you face unnecessary inconvenience. The easy way to prevent all these mistakes is to check back on last year's returns. Compare both the documents to eliminate the risk of a typo when manually entering your information.

Mathematical Mistakes: Tax forms use mathematical formulas that are known to be tricky. For instance, "Add line 9 to line 31 and multiply the sum by .356 if your AGI is more than $50,000." Calculations like these can make tax returns a scary task for those of us who had a hard time in math class. Save yourself from making simple mistakes on these calculations and use an online tax returns preparation software that automatically does the math for you. There are various tax preparing apps out there; all you must do is answer simple questions and add the basic numbers you already have. The software will do the rest of the work for you and save you time.

Not Staying Updated With Tax News: The tax laws not only are complicated, but governmental bodies make alterations in it almost every year. The tax reform in the last months of 2017 was the most significant overhaul of tax laws in nearly 30 years. This much change is undoubtedly overwhelming. You should certainly get in touch with your tax-collecting agency or tax news for essential updates. This way, you will not miss out on any valuable deductions, credits or attempts to claim tax benefits that do not exist anymore.

Not Safe-keeping a Copy of Your Return After Filing: Tax advisors recommend keeping copies of your tax return with yourself for at least three years. Three years is only the minimum time; you should ideally keep tax returns for life. But three years is how long tax collectors can legally investigate you for under-reporting your income. Fortunately, you can print and recheck your tax returns for up to seven years.

Entering Incorrect Account Numbers: Double-checking your bank account and routing numbers is always a must-do if you want to make sure the refund direct is deposited or if you are paying your tax online. Entering the incorrect account number does not mean your money will be wasted. Still, it can delay the refund or result in fines and interest charges on late payments.

Missing a Tax Break: Tax collecting agencies like the IRS are very generous; however, some tax credits and exemptions available still available– especially for students and families. Credits like Child Tax Credit and the sort can decrease your taxes by as much as $2,000, so make certain that you never miss out on any exemptions or credits for which you qualify. You should always think twice before making a decision to choose the standard deduction. Homeowners, particularly, should enlist their most significant deductions to check if they sum up to more than the standard amount.

Filing the Wrong Tax Forms: The IRS is now offering a single income tax form for all the filers regardless of the tax situation: Form 1040. The forms 1040A and 1040EZ were discarded when the tax year 2018 started. The updates in Form 1040 also brought along six new schedules.

Filing Under The Incorrect Status: The IRS will apply various income tax rates and award different standard deductions depending on your filing status. The different filing statuses are; single, married joint-filing, married separate filing, head of the house, or qualifying widow or widower. Married couples jointly filing, for instance, receive two times the standard deduction received by unmarried filers. You should also note that if you are married but filing separately, you are subject to different rules and regulations than joint filers. For example, filing separately, both partners are required to claim the standard or itemized deductions but not both. Figuring out your tax bracket can be tough sometimes, so you can use any online tax bracket calculator to find out.

Not Filing in the First Place: Even if you are unable to pay the full amount of your tax bill at the due time, you should always file a return and get in touch with the IRS to initiate a payment plan. In an instalment payment plan, the interest rates are lower, so it is much better than not foiling at all, which will result in higher interest rates on the tax debt, fines and even tax evasion charges against you.

www.ingramcontent.com/pod-product-compliance
Lightning Source LLC
Chambersburg PA
CBHW021444210526
45463CB00002B/628